# The Writing-Rich High School Classroom

### Engaging Students in the Writing Workshop

Jennifer Berne

THE GUILFORD PRESS
New York    London

© 2009 The Guilford Press
A Division of Guilford Publications, Inc.
72 Spring Street, New York, NY 10012
www.guilford.com

Printed in the United States of America

This book is printed on acid-free paper.

Last digit is print number:   9   8   7   6   5   4   3   2   1

**Library of Congress Cataloging-in-Publication Data**

Berne, Jennifer.
    The writing-rich high school classroom : engaging students in the writing
workshop / Jennifer Berne.
        p.   cm.
    Includes bibliographical references and index.
    ISBN 978-1-60623-024-4 (hardcover: alk. paper)
    ISBN 978-1-60623-023-7 (pbk.: alk. paper)
    1. English language—Composition and exercises—Study and teaching
(Secondary)   2. English language—Rhetoric—Study and teaching
(Secondary)   I. Title.
    LB1631.B394 2009
    808'.0420712—dc22

                                                                    2008038830

# About the Author

Jennifer Berne, PhD, has been a writing teacher and an educator of writing teachers for 20 years. She began her career as a community college writing instructor, working with struggling readers and writers. Dr. Berne is currently Assistant Professor and Chair of Reading and Language at National-Louis University in Wheeling, Illinois. In addition to teaching and researching, she is a consultant to numerous school districts on the implementation and support of writing process instruction. She can be reached at Jennifer.Berne@nl.edu.

# Contents

# CHAPTER ONE

# The High School
# Writing Workshop

Of all the writing I have done, none has been more difficult than writing the first chapter of a book about the teaching of writing. It is terrifying. If my writing is not clear, how could I possibly teach anyone how to teach about writing with clarity? If my writing is disorganized, will you believe even one thing I have to say about helping students to organize their writing? And, worst of all, what if I make a grammatical error? Working through these anxieties has taught me much about writing. Putting fear aside to get down to what I want to say reminds me of the significant courage all writers muster when sharing their writing. It is understanding that courage that propels me forward. Students often write little and share little of their writing because they are afraid of the consequences. They are afraid of low grades or of presenting themselves poorly. They may also be afraid of being misunderstood, of having an idea that they cannot communicate effectively. Although young children scribble and create with great joy, once students reach high school, they often face writing tasks with anxiety and the resulting experience can be painful.

The same can be said for the teaching of writing. Many of us went into teaching because we loved our subject and wanted to share that love with others. The prospect of helping people embrace new ideas and express their thoughts about them leads many toward a career in education. The prospect of learning about students through their writing is exciting and privileged—there are few professions that pay us to read stories. However that initial thrill can be squelched when we are confronted with hundreds of students representing thousands of pages of writing that can weigh down and defeat even the most devoted among us.

This configuration—students' fear or disdain for writing, coupled with teachers' rightful claim to reasonable parameters for a life of their own—has caused the teaching of writing and, consequently, the learning of writing to suffer. This is not a new problem. Teachers bemoaning responding to students' writing and students bemoaning writing altogether has a long history in literacy education. I make no promises that all students will fall in love with writing or that all teachers will ask to teach their whole load in composition, but there are ways to think about both that can bring more intrigue and joy into teaching and learning about writing.

This book describes the creation of a writing classroom centered on teaching the process of writing. Many books about the teaching of writing are organized by genre. In these books you will find techniques for teaching genres such as narrative, expository, argumentative, fiction, research, and, high-stakes test writing. Other books about the teaching of writing are organized by trait. In books like these you will find well-established practices for teaching students about voice, organization, audience awareness, word choice, and correct grammar. Some of these books are referenced in the chapters to come, and many have influenced high school writers in productive ways. Teachers who use books like these to prepare themselves to teach writing to students often arrange their classes to mirror one of these structures. They may spend a few weeks focusing on writing in one or another genre, or they may organize around traits and spend time helping students understand and practice these. This book suggests an alternative structure in that it asks teachers to focus on the process of writing as the curriculum. When organizing a class around process, students learn about genre and traits for certain, but they do so by working on their writing and learning what it means to use a process. Teachers break apart the pieces of the writing process and give students experience in strategies for managing each piece. Although it is true that writing cannot always be broken down into discrete stages, it is necessary for students to do this as they learn about each stage. Once they achieve some confidence in the stages, they might never again think of them as quite this discrete. When writers approach simple tasks that they do all the time, they rarely pay attention to the stages in explicit ways. They just write. However when they approach more difficult writing tasks, they need to know what they can do when the writing doesn't come as easily—how they will start, how they will use feedback, how they will edit. It is experience in these stages in the community of a writing classroom that allows writers to handle these more difficult tasks.

Most teachers are familiar with the components of the writing process—planning, drafting, revising, giving and receiving feedback, editing, and publishing. But many are not accustomed to using these components as the curriculum for their writing classroom. This book is about how to teach students to understand and use the writing process to improve their writing in all genres and in all traits.

Teaching the writing process, sometimes called the writing workshop approach, is less a set of practices than a philosophy or stance about the way that students learn to write. This "writing process stance" comprises the following tenets:

- *Students learn to write by writing.* In the writing workshop, students write a lot. Some writing is worked on over a period of time. Some of the writing is written and immediately forgotten. Much of the writing students do in the writing workshop is shared with peers or the teacher for feedback, but not all.

- *Learning to revise is learning to write.* Learning to revise, literally re-see, one's writing is key to the writing workshop and commands much time and attention. Writing fluently and fast is great, and writers learn from doing so. Writing fluently and fast and then stepping back and giving the writing time to sit and/or getting feedback from others teaches writers about the effect of their writing on an audience. Skill in writing comes from hard work and lots of feedback. Learning to revise is about learning how to use feedback.

- *Students learn to write by writing about what they care about.* There are always times when writing assignments are dictated from outside. Students will need to learn how to write to a task or a prompt. Real progress in writing, however, comes from investing in a topic. To be authors, students must have authority over their own work. This authority should start with control over content whenever possible. When students are invested in their message, instruction in delivery of that message is far more potent than instruction given when a student is writing to fulfill an obligation.

- *Student writing should be both good and correct.* So much of writing instruction in elementary and middle grades is concerned with conforming to rules of Standard Written English. Of course it is important to equip students with the tools necessary to participate in all levels of education and the outside world. Correctness is a necessary condition for proficiency in writing, but it is not sufficient on its own. To be skilled at writing, students must know how to write both correctly and well. Correct writing is error free; good writing is filled with life. It has a message, a voice, and it offers the reader something. That something could be information, humor, pleasure, anger, or sadness. This "something" is what makes writing good. The goal in writing instruction should be to help students to work at writing that is both correct and good.

- *Students should be assessed by their growth in using the writing process and by the resulting product.* Success in a writing course should be based both on how the student works through the writing process and on the outcome of that process. When students learn a new skill, they don't always progress magically from less skill to more skill. In learning writing, there may be many bumps along the way as students learn how to handle increasingly difficult writing tasks or try out new strategies. Students in writing workshops are rewarded for final products but also for evidence that they know how to use strategies even if those strategies don't always result in expert writing.

## Contextualizing Writing Process Instruction

It is commonly believed that Janet Emig's (1971) study of the composition habits of high school students helped kick-start the paradigm shift in writing instruction. Emig described the teaching of writing in high schools particularly harshly as "a neurotic activity" and set out to learn why she believed it to be ineffective. Her descriptive case studies of excellent high school writers helped to illuminate the chasm between school writing and "real" writing. Using a think-aloud protocol (a process by which people are asked to articulate their thoughts as they engage in an activity so that an understanding of their thinking process emerges to those listening) to help understand the writing process of secondary students, Emig noted the differences between the way students planned and executed writing in schools and the way they approached nonrequired writing. Extrapolating from this information, Emig and other scholars began to describe the writing processes of proficient writers and contrasting them to those of less-proficient writers. From this contrast emerged a theoretical model of writing as a set of stages, not always discrete, not always obvious, but stages nonetheless. This idea that writing was a set of stages and that learning to write may be a matter of practice with the stages, set educators up to think about writing instruction in new ways.

Although process writing instruction may have developed because of research done with high school students, its place in secondary education has never been secure. In the late 1980s and early 1990s, elementary education programs began to introduce preservice teachers to the concepts and practices associated with process writing. This involved a significant shift for teacher educators and teacher education students because this instruction was not consistent with their own experience learning to write in school. As in all paradigm shifts, there was significant push–pull through many years, but process writing is now a commonly accepted practice in K–5 literacy education. This is not the case for high school writers. Other notions of how to teach writing (e.g., rhetorical structures, authorial models) predominate in high schools and in many cases are the only models taught by high school teachers.

Scholars believe there to be no age or grade boundaries to this kind process writing instruction. In fact much of the initial push toward writing workshops came from university freshman composition courses where college-level instructors attempted to find ways to remedy the woodenness of student writing (see, e.g., Macrorie, 1976; Bartholomae & Petrosky, 1986). Still, though, little has trickled up from elementary or down from university to influence process writing theory and practice in high school writing instruction. It is now time to consider for secondary students all the innovations in writing that have served student writers in other grades so well.

## Stages in the Writing Process

Donald Graves (1983) was among the first to isolate the stages of writing and identify them in linear order. Along with his student Lucy Calkins, Graves helped to describe "the writing process." To Graves the stages were planning, drafting, revising, editing, and publishing. Identifying and naming the stages was a major milestone because it drew attention to the parts that made the whole. I draw heavily on these stages, but I also unpack some of them and subdivide them into portions that, in my experience, need different kinds of classroom attention. In this book

**TABLE 1.1. Writing Process Stages, Comparing Graves (1983) to the Stages Described in This Book**

| Graves's writing process stages | Graves unpacked |
| --- | --- |
| Planning | Prewriting<br>Planning |
| Drafting | Drafting |
| Revision | Giving and receiving feedback<br>Revision |
| Editing | Editing<br>Proofreading |
| Publishing | Publishing |

you'll find the writing process as described by attention to prewriting, planning, drafting, giving and receiving feedback, revision, editing, proofreading, and publishing. For a graphic of these stages and how they relate to the stages described by Graves, see Table 1.1.

## Understanding the Structure of This Book

Corresponding to this structure are the elements of this book. This book is divided into chapters that focus on setting up a classroom in which the stages in the writing process are the primary curriculum.

• Chapter 2 is a discussion of how to set students up to be successful in the writing workshop. It includes suggestions for the first weeks of class, especially in preparing students for the cognitive and social demands of the writing workshop. In addition, the structure of classroom days, classroom weeks, and cycles of writing instruction are detailed.

• Chapter 3 describes the kinds of assignments most meaningful for students working in the writing workshop and also what genres and types of writing are best worked on outside the boundaries of the writing workshop.

• Chapter 4 begins the sections devoted to stages of the writing process. In this chapter, prewriting and planning strategies and structures are discussed.

- Chapter 5 discusses drafting. First-draft writing is often called drafting. Once this was the whole of what writing was in writing classrooms. In this model, drafting is one, albeit important, element in the process of writing.
- Chapter 6 begins the first of three chapters on revising writing. Teaching revision is key in teaching students how to improve their writing, yet this element is often missing in writing courses. This chapter presents an incremental approach to teaching revision, one that scaffolds students in their learning before they are ready to experiment with many different revision techniques.
- Chapter 7 discusses the vital role of peer feedback in writing process instruction. Peer feedback is essential, yet students unprepared to give and use peer feedback will find this activity useless and frustrating. This chapter offers concrete suggestions for improving students' ability to give feedback to one another and to use the feedback peers give them.
- Chapter 8 discusses how teachers can be efficient and effective in their feedback. Students need preparation in how to listen to verbal feedback from teachers and how to read written feedback from teachers. Once students know how to do this, teacher feedback will be far more useful than if students are left to interpret comments unassisted. Teachers will abandon any kind of teaching that is impractical because of time constraints; thus this chapter gives suggestions for a realistic time frame for responding.
- Chapter 9 describes a model for teaching correctness in writing process classrooms. Editing is distinct from revision in writing workshop, but it is no less important. Once students have created papers that are good, they must know how to make them correct. Discussed are strategies for identifying and correcting grammatical, mechanical, and spelling errors.
- Chapter 10 offers ideas for summative evaluation for student writing and for managing the relationship between formative and summative feedback on student work.

## Buzzwords: Technology, Differentiation, and Assessment

This book offers secondary teachers a structure for teaching writing rather than an examination of what constitutes fine writing. Because of this, particular instructional elements are embedded in discussions of pieces of the process rather than discussed individually in their own chapters. For instance, technology is used very differently in drafting than it is in the editing process, so those discussions are embedded in the chapters on drafting and editing. Technological changes have influenced many aspects of the writing workshop, but none as dramatically as the publication of student work. Computer technology has altered the way student writing can appear on a page, and it has greatly increased the opportunities for students to "publish" or share their work with a broad audience if they so choose or are directed by a teacher to do so. For this reason, the discussion of new technologies available in the service of teaching writing has been centered in the chapter on evaluation, where the discussion of publishing student work is presented.

Differentiation is handled similarly. Writing instruction is self-differentiating, meaning that we can hand students of diverse abilities the same writing tasks, and they will be able to handle the tasks at their own developmental level. This is characteristic of process writing instruction and one of its most important contributions to students' literacy. It is possible to hand a student a book during reading instruction, for instance, that is so far above or below his or her reading ability as to be useless in instruction. If it is too easy, the student knows it so well that he or she doesn't require classroom help to understand its meaning. If it is far too difficult, no amount of classroom intervention may make much difference. But when handed a writing task, students will write what they can at their own level of sophistication. They can't create something beyond their own understanding, and we help them learn not to write something so simple that it isn't worthy of effort. Thus, differentiation in writing ability, in gender, in social class, in race, and in first language is not handled in a chapter about differences. The writing process is about students' individual writing, and in some sense their differences. This book is always addressing differentiation in writing. Students start from where they are and progress. No two students will start and end at the same place.

Because assessment is largely holistic in writing process classrooms (although there can certainly be explicit attention to individual traits of writing and/or student achievement in specific portions of the process) it was not sensible to include a discussion of assessment in individual chapters. Thus assessment is woven throughout the chapter on teacher feedback (i.e., formative feedback) and the chapter on evaluation (i.e., the summative mark).

## Engaging in Conversation

This book is based on my beliefs about writing, teaching, and learning. I believe there is an abundance of rich discussions of writing instruction directed toward elementary and middle school teachers. I draw significantly on these books, particularly those by Ralph Fletcher (1993, 2004), Donald Graves (1983, 1994), Lucy Calkins (1994, 2006), Nancie Atwell (1998), and Regie Routman (1991, 1996). I am also influenced by the significant work in college-level writing instruction and theory discussed by Peter Elbow (1973, 1981), Donald Murray (1996), David Bartholomae (Bartholomae & Petrosky, 1986), Nancy Sommers (1982), and Mike Rose (Rose, 1989). Many of these scholars are cited throughout this text. I urge you to read their work as you continue to develop your own theory of what works in the teaching of writing. I wish to add to the conversations that I engage in with and among these thinkers and writers by instantiating these theories in the practical life of a high school writing teacher.

CHAPTER TWO

# Setting Up and Managing the Writing Workshop

Compared with traditional instructional models, the writing workshop appears unstructured and casual. Students flourish because of the independence offered in the writing workshop, but this independent activity requires significant behind-the-scenes preparation. Teachers prepare students to participate in the writing workshop for many weeks before knowing that they can function appropriately. The best, most productive writing workshops take place in environments where students observe standards and adhere to processes that minimize off-task behavior, freeing them for the significant creative and cognitive task of writing well. Lucy Calkins describes her own epiphany relative to setting up structures and processes for learning how to write:

> I have finally realized that the most creative environments in our society are not the kaleidoscopic environments in which everything is always changing and complex. They are, instead, the predictable and consistent ones—the scholar's library, the researcher's laboratory, the artist's studio. Each of these environments is deliberately kept predictable and simple because the work at hand and the changing interactions around that work are so unpredictable and complex. (1983, p. 32)

You'll find that students of all levels need time and practice to prepare for the activities necessary for productive writing workshops.

## Getting Off to the Best Possible Start

It may seem daunting, but you'll find that careful up-front preparation and continual monitoring and refinement through the first several weeks of class are critical to minimize disruptions, help students to focus, and thus reap the long-term benefits of writing workshop.

Because the writing workshop's focus on individual responsibility is different from the traditional classroom experience, students need help to adjust. Writing teachers from elementary school through college have found that there are no shortcuts to helping students understand how to function socially (by using time wisely) and physically (by being where they ought to be) in this environment so that they can function cognitively as writers engaged in the craft. In order to succeed in this, students need explicit instruction in what to do and how to do it. This setting-up period can take as long as a month, and even after that month students may require periodic tune-ups in the form of reminders, further modeling, and mini-lessons on acceptable and unacceptable behaviors.

By the end of September you may be tempted to put your head down on your desk, wondering whether you will ever get to teach students about their writing. If so, you are not alone. Most teachers experience impatience as they launch the writing workshop. You'll have to trust that the sacrifice of time and energy is tolerable, because using that time to build structure and clarify activities allows for little interruption once this period is over. Front-loaded preparation that includes significant modeling, practice, and troubleshooting of what to do, when to do it, and how to do it helps keep your writing workshop productive. Teachers who don't prepare up front may see their workshops morphing into a giant mass of activity without clear direction. Advocates of the writing workshop have watched their colleagues try to "begin in the middle" of this kind of instruction, neglecting to provide appropriate and significant preparation for students. These teachers almost inevitably abandon the practice in favor of one that is more teacher centered, insisting that students cannot work with this much independence. Counterexamples exist across the grade levels, where students do work productively and independently, if not 100% of the time, at least for an acceptable portion. When you listen to teachers in these kinds of classrooms describe their process of preparing students, it is consistently a matter of high expectations, significant practice, and ongoing feedback on how students are behaving and how they are writing. It *is* worth the effort.

Teachers who have never experienced writing process as students, and may never have observed it, will have to rely upon the experiences of veteran teachers of writing workshop for a while, until they find their own rhythm and ways. In your zeal to get on with it and experience the pleasures of watching student writers grow, you may be tempted to skip or to go too quickly through these important steps— steps that, although not part of the writing process per se, are definitely part of the writing process *classroom*. As you read, be sure to refer to the *How's It Done?* boxes that you will find in this chapter and in those that follow. In these you will find the experiences of veteran writing process teachers, and particularly the schedules, templates, and other resources that have helped them to manage this work. The first *How's It Done?* box shows a calendar used by one ninth-grade teacher to plan the first 3 weeks of her writing workshop, a time she devotes exclusively to helping students ready themselves for the workshop ahead. In this chapter and the ones that follow, all teacher and student names are pseudonyms.

## Organizing Your Physical Space

Students in traditional classrooms often require specific directions when they are asked to move out of their seats for group or paired activities, but in the fluid environment of the writing workshop, students are always moving and need to do so on their own initiative. The writing workshop was initially modeled after fine-arts courses. In courses like painting and sculpture, the instructor might talk with the students for a short time, but his or her primary role is to circulate among the students as they work to provide feedback and guidance. Likewise you'll seldom find yourself in the traditional front-of-the-room pose while students are in a writing workshop. Although this may be new for you, it is also very new for your students. They may be accustomed to this in the shop room and the gymnasium, even the science laboratory, but seldom in English. However, traditional classroom setups do not lend themselves to the kind of activities students will do in a writing workshop. Even if the teacher can negotiate through rows of student desks, the collaborative nature of the writing workshop makes rows of stu-

## How's It Done?: Scheduling the First 3 Weeks

Ms. P knew her 10th-grade students would not be used to all the freedom and responsibility required to work most productively in her writing workshop. She also knew that even the most dedicated students might struggle with the cognitive challenges. In response, she planned a 3-week "training" period. This training period included instruction in how writers get the most from this time. Since Ms. P planned to have students work in writing workshop on Mondays, Wednesdays, and Fridays in 3-week chunks, her training period would follow that same schedule as summarized below.

This calendar notes training directed at students' work in a peer response group. This is often the activity that needs the most practice. These activities range in duration: some take the whole class period and others are over with class time to spare. When Ms. P has time, she also models activities related to planning, drafting, editing, and getting and using teacher feedback.

Ms. P believes this to be time well spent because students are learning about behaviors as they are also learning how to pick out the elements of strong writing and identify what would improve a paper.

| Sept. 1 | Sept. 3 | Sept. 5 |
|---|---|---|
| Introduce idea of writing workshop. Ask students to think about the reasons people write, the difficulties, and what is most pleasurable. Show students a visual of stages of the writing process. | Tell students that the hardest part of this is managing the peer response process and that they are going to learn how to behave and what to say. Show anchor chart of desirable and nondesirable behaviors. Show them where in the room they will go for the peer response group, where to sign up for it, and how long it should be. | Invite four adults to come to the room and model. Have adults and students write for 10 minutes. Prompt: Talk about a time when your experience didn't match your expectation. Adults participate in peer group as students watch and comment. |

*(continued)*

| Sept. 8 | Sept. 10 | Sept. 12 |
|---|---|---|
| Debrief further about adult example. What did they do well? What could they do better? Read teacher response and ask students to respond in the whole group as they would in the small group. | Place students in groups of four or five at random. Ask them just to go around the table and read their responses. Each person should be told something nice about his/her paper, so students get used to reading and listening before they are ready to attempt substantive feedback. | Show students a videotape of other students working in a group (from last year) and have them comment. |
| Sept. 15 | Sept. 17 | Sept. 19 |
| Ask four students to volunteer to read their work and get feedback while the rest of the class observes and, when they are through, comments. | Ask students to write for only 5 minutes. Prompt: Something you recall struggling to learn to do. Put them in groups of four or five and have them respond to these very short pieces. Every student should get at least one piece of usable feedback. | Reflect back on all activities to remind students what is and what is not a productive group. Tell students they will begin to use this process with their writing next week when the writing workshop begins. |

dents sitting at their desks a barrier to the work. Most high schools are not equipped with rooms designed solely as workshops, so you will have to shift the furniture for this period and save a minute or two at the end of the workshop to reassemble the room for the next period if writing workshop is not the only course you teach.

Students may be planning their writing, drafting, getting and giving feedback, revising, or editing during the writing workshop. Each of these activities will need to be staged in a different location within your room. This helps facilitate your role of advisor and also the important activities involved in student collaboration.

### Student Desks

Ideally, student desks are separated somewhat to allow for teacher circulation, paired consultations among students, and some measure of privacy when desired. Students generally work on planning, drafting, and revising at their own desk, as these tend to be individual activities.

### Peer Response Areas

Two areas are needed for two different kinds of collaborative activities. One, a peer response area, can be space on the floor or at a table, with enough space for multiple groups of four or five students to meet. Another space should be for collaborative or group editing. This table or area on the floor should be distinct from the peer response area to emphasize the different nature of the two tasks. Students (and sometimes teachers) have a good deal of trouble distinguishing the activities of feedback to prompt revision and collaborative editing support. Untangling these activities by physically separating them secures the difference in students' minds. Finally, students will meet with the teacher in a writing conference either at the teacher's desk—in which case a student space is needed—or by the teacher moving to the student desk—in which case a teacher space is needed.

## Finding Space for Word Processing

Word processing has been shown to have a positive influence on student writing (Graham & Perin, 2007). Even without a computer for every student, word processing can be integrated into the writing workshop (see Chapter 5 for a fuller discussion of using computer word-processing technology to support the writing process). If computers are available, students will move to them during drafting, after feedback as they begin revision, and after collaborative editing support as they prepare their paper for publication. Unless laptops are available for students' use at their own desks or tables, they will have to move to the computer area to work on these activities. Laptop carts or computer labs can also be integrated into the space needed to work on writing. Teachers should not be discouraged from supporting student writing with technology merely because they do not have a computer available for every student.

You can and should take measures beforehand to regulate how you would like students to move when they are ready to engage in a new part of the writing process. Because student movement can be chaotic, teachers will regulate, in their own way, how they would like students to move. Is all movement silent? Do students first put their name in a slot at the front of the room indicating where they will move and for what purpose? Teachers have devised many strategies for keeping student whereabouts under control. It is important that students show that they are moving through the writing process both physically and cognitively. A sample log that you may consider using to keep track of student activity is presented later in this chapter. Other teachers prefer to put all student names on magnets or clothespins and have the students move their name to the slot corresponding with the portion of the writing process in which they are engaged. A graphic of this can be found in Figure 2.1.

## Preparing Students for Participation

The most important preparation you can provide for writing workshop students is to help them learn to collaborate on their work. Having an audience provided for a writer and being an audience for other writers are among the most important components of the writing workshop, yet these are not intuitive activities for most students. Students need

| Ready for: | Ready for: | Ready for: |
|---|---|---|
| Peer group | Teacher conference | Written response |
| Caroline | Sophie | Kayla |
| Justin | Trejaun | George |
| Alicia | Kristine | Juan |
| Roman | | Tia |

**FIGURE 2.1.** Sign-up sheets.

careful, planned instruction in the behaviors necessary to encourage success in giving and receiving feedback. They need to know how to handle too much or too little feedback and how to respond to wanted and unwanted commentary. Chapters 7 and 8 provide suggested strategies on how to support students in giving and receiving feedback as part of the writing process. This includes how to be a good responder and writing partner and how to use advice given by a peer. These skills alone, however, won't help students become better writers if they do not know how to handle themselves in the classroom. Off-task behavior will derail both weak and strong students, and the whole purpose of this setting-up time is to minimize this problem. Many secondary teachers spend a better part of the first weeks of class explaining the structures in the writing process, modeling how one moves around, setting up opportunities for guided practice, giving support, and helping students move toward independence in the social, physical, and cognitive tasks before them.

## Kicking Off with Mini-Lessons

A mini-lesson is a short piece of whole-group instruction that can introduce a strategy or behavior you want to cultivate. The writing workshop almost always begins with a mini-lesson. As time progresses and students become more comfortable in the workshop, you'll likely focus these lessons on characteristics of good writing and strategies for improving writing. In the beginning, though, you will want to focus these lessons on being a member of a writing workshop classroom. Some of these initial mini-lessons might include how to know when you have a complete first draft, where to go to get feedback, when to go to the teacher, when and where to edit, or what to do if you finish your work. You will be the best person to determine which physical or cognitive tasks need the most rehearsal for your students. Thus you might find that students have no difficulty getting up from their desk and moving quietly to the peer review table. You also might find that students need a visual image of doing this in a respectful, nondisruptive manner. If they can use this support, a mini-lesson is a good way to do it.

The total time the mini-lesson takes should be brief (thus the name mini-lesson), because it is important for students to get short bursts of information, have the task or behavior modeled, practice it with guidance, and then begin to move toward independence. Below are the steps and suggested language to use as a heuristic for a mini-lesson focused on one writing element. This mini-lesson structure is designed so that teachers can plug in any topic they deem appropriate for students so that the instruction is consistently presented. In the interest of showing, and not telling, however, an actual mini-lesson scenario is listed below. The structure for mini-lessons is summarized in Figure 2.2.

### Introduce the Task or Objective

"Today we are going to talk about how writers use their writer's notebook to come up with ideas for writing. This activity is a part of prewriting and is important because it prepares the writer the way that an athlete might stretch before competing in a sport or a chef might gather his ingredients before preparing a dish. Writers use their notebook to experiment with lots of ideas; sometimes we call these 'seeds' of ideas. When you have a number of seeds, it is great to look through them, to reread and see what you have written. Often one of them pops up as having the most potential for further writing. Sometimes none pop out dramatically, so writers just select one that they continue to work with. This is very low risk, and that what is great about it. If you begin writing with a seed and determine it isn't going anywhere, you can look back at your notebook and see what else is there."

### Talk about How Students Get Started

"I have provided you each with a writer's notebook. For the rest of this week, we are going to begin class by writing about something that you saw recently, something you did recently, or something

| First step | Introduce the task or objective. |
|---|---|
| Second step | Talk about how students get started. |
| Third step | Model the process for students. |
| Fourth step | Lead students in practicing the process. |
| Fifth step | Debrief the whole group. |
| Sixth step | Prepare students for the physical, cognitive, and social demands of working independently. |

**FIGURE 2.2.** Mini-lesson template.

you wondered about recently. We are going to try to get several pages of writing for each entry. At the end of the week we will have many pages of writing that, ideally, will generate more ideas for our writing."

## Model the Process for Students

You can choose to model on chart paper, an overhead, document camera, or the chalkboard. Some processes need to be physically acted out. You may consider a think-aloud, sharing with students what you are thinking as you write. Then you might reflect together on the modeling that has just occurred.

> "I was thinking as I was coming into work this morning that this change in the weather bothers me much more than it did years ago. I think I am going to write about how that change might be indicative of other changes. [*Teacher writes.*] As I get older I know I am less flexible; even small alterations in my style throw me for a loop. Will I ever be able to roll with the punches as I used to. . . . [Teacher continues to think aloud and write for up to 5 minutes as students watch.] OK, students, what did you just see and hear me do?"

## Lead Students in Practicing the Process

> "OK, now I am going to have you open your writer's notebook and make a few quick entries. You don't have to write a lot about any one thing, and if you need a prompt I have provided you with a list inside your notebook." [For a list of prompts, see Chapter 4.]

## Debrief the Whole Group

> "What did it feel like to write in this way? What difficulties did you have? Let's remind ourselves why we might do this on a regular basis."

## Prepare Students for the Physical, Cognitive, and Social Demands of Doing This Independently

> "Now, often you are going to be working in your writer's notebook independently of the rest of the class. For instance during the writ-

ing workshop you may be waiting for me to come conference with you or waiting for a group of your peers to be ready to hold a peer response group. These are times to begin entries in your notebook, to look back at old ones, to see whether these are ripe for continuation. When you have moments that are not taken up by a writing project, this is where you turn. We will do some whole-group writing in our notebooks, and I will sometimes also ask you to make entries outside of this class. Today, however, I want you to think of using it as writing practice when other writing you are doing is put on hold as you wait for others. Let's try it. Here is the scenario: You are doing some writing and come to the point where you just don't know where else to go. You see that there is a sign-up sheet for a peer editing group with one other name on it. Because you know that you must have four students to make a group, you put your name on and return to your desk to wait. As you wait, you pull out your writer's notebook and begin writing or rereading past entries. When you note that other students are ready for the peer response group, you finish the point or sentence you are on, put your notebook away, and begin working on the piece you wanted feedback on in order to continue to improve. This is the correct way to use a writer's notebook. What are some of the things you expect would not be appropriate? [Teacher lists these—e.g., looking at someone's notebook without permission, taking it home and not bringing it back, doing other homework while waiting to go to the peer group, bothering other students who are writing, discussing nonwriting concerns with peers.]"

This mini-lesson is not the end of the discussion/modeling/practice on using a writer's notebook. Mini-lessons are not intended as the sole instruction in anything. They are little bursts of instruction that may be repeated to students in individual or small-group conversations or in future whole-group instruction. At times you may notice that students are not participating in one part of writing workshop as they once did, or they are disrupting other students. This would be a time for a tune-up mini-lesson reinforcing appropriate and inappropriate behaviors when engaging in this structure. When you are ready to introduce editing, revision, feedback, and publishing you may do similarly structured lessons. Mini-lessons such as this one are designed to help students gain insight on how writers work and to observe a more expert writer engaged in that process. These strategies also help to establish good habits that can be sustained throughout the year. Chapter 5 offers further ideas for mini-lessons related to specific qualities of writing. This structure for mini-lessons is based on the gradual-release model introduced by Pearson and Gallagher (1983).

The gradual-release model requires that you demonstrate a process by cognitively and/or physically modeling it for your students. You then guide students in the practice and ask them to reflect on what they have done. Finally, you set up opportunities for practice that will become increasingly independent.

A template for mini-lessons is important for classroom structure and for teacher ease. Students are introduced to the structure so that it is transparent. You and your students adhere to a predictable structure for mini-lessons, and teachers need not reinvent the wheel every time they share a mini-lesson with students.

These kinds of process mini-lessons occupy much of the first month as students learn about the writing workshop. Once students understand and have practiced some of the basic practices and understandings, content-focused mini-lessons are introduced. These can follow the same pattern as the process mini-lessons but might focus on adding details, organizing writing, or combining sentences to increase writing fluency. Teachers generally use their students' writing to determine what aspects of instruction would be most beneficial. Sometimes you might differentiate these lessons by pulling a portion of the class and working with them on one concept for which not everyone is ready. It is important to note that a mini-lesson offers no magic. Any task that is challenging enough for students that it requires a mini-lesson will probably require more than one. Each mini-lesson need not be unique, and teachers may decide to focus on just a few concepts for a period of weeks or months. A full discussion of grammar mini-lessons appears in Chapter 9.

## Scaffolding Student Collaboration

Students spend a great deal of their time in writing workshop conferring with one another or with you. This presents two interrelated management concerns—students must be able to work together productively, and they must do so without your watchful eye, as you will likely be busy in conference with one of their peers. Nobody believes that adolescents will attend to their schoolwork 100% of the time without significant instruction in strategies for staying on task. It will be necessary for you to model appropriate behavior, discuss inappropriate behavior, manufacture scenarios in which students must decide how to handle disruptions, and in some cases work out a system for tracking levels of productive participation. You may want to give points for every day that students meet a level of productivity, or simply deduct points or lower grades when students are off task. It may take experimentation to determine what works. You may want to consider using a log like the one provided in Figure 2.3 to help you track and record student locations and behaviors.

This weekly log can help you monitor where students are in the process and easily see whether they are at the appropriate location. You might ask students to fill out the "location" and "activities" column, perhaps on a piece of chart paper or a whiteboard, and then you can note absences and areas for concern. For example Amanda marked herself at her own desk coming up with ideas, yet when her teacher looked up she found her to be otherwise engaged. Recording documents of this type can be helpful because they track students' progress through the process. Even if Amanda's teacher were unaware that she was off track (because, for example, she was sitting at her desk quietly doing nothing), she could immediately note that a whole week is too long to be coming up with ideas. Her knowledge of Amanda and her work habits would suggest to her whether Amanda might be really stuck, in

| Student | Week of 2/14 | Location(s) | Activities | Assessment |
|---------|--------------|-------------|------------|------------|
| Megan | | Desk<br>Peer review table | Drafting<br>Feedback | OK |
| Tori | Absent<br>Monday | Desk | Planning | |
| Jake | | Teacher desk<br>Editing table | Conference | OK |
| Rhianna | | Computer lab<br>Other student<br>desk | Drafting<br>Buddy response | OK |
| Jorge | | Peer review table<br>Desk | Feedback<br>Revision | OK |
| Amanda | | Desk | Coming up with<br>ideas | ✓ Unacceptable |
| Stephen | | Computer lab | Final draft<br>Publishing | OK |

**FIGURE 2.3.** Sample student tracking form.

which case she may need some teacher support, or whether she is using her time unwisely.

Regardless of how teachers prepare students for participation, this is not an element that can be skipped. Careful planning of management and practicing of desirable behaviors will ensure the best chance for successful writing workshops.

## Scheduling and Sequencing the Writing Workshop

In the chapters that follow, we explore how the writing workshop can coexist with and complement other forms of writing instruction. For now it is enough to say that a minimum amount of time dedicated entirely to the writing workshop is required for long-term effect on student writing. Because high school writing/language arts/English classes typically span only one period, it is recommended that at least 2 of the 5 days that the course meets should be devoted to the writing workshop. Many teachers spend 3 or even 4 days and find that works best for them. Novice teachers are wise to ease into this more slowly to explore the benefits of the writing workshop and also what it doesn't do. You should plan to spend 40 minutes per session on the writing workshop; thus high school classes that aren't in large blocks of time will likely do very little else on writing workshop days. While many teachers select 2 or 3 days a week to do the writing workshop for the entire quarter, semester, or year, others prefer to do the workshop every day for a period of time, say 3 weeks, and then focus on other aspects of literacy, perhaps even including genres of writing that are more efficiently taught in a context other than the writing workshop (e.g., standardized test writing) for another chunk of time. In this model, students participate in the workshop for a period of weeks, then use those skills to enhance other literacy activities, in turn using skills from those other literacy activities to fold back into the writing workshop when it starts up again.

For example you might begin with students writing a narrative, expository, or argumentative paper, instructing them as they go through the stages of the writing process. If students do this each time the course meets for 2 or 3 weeks, many of the students will have produced a finished draft ready for publication by the end of that time. The next 2- or 3-week chunk might be devoted to a specialized genre of writing, high-stakes test taking for example, that doesn't lend itself as comfortably to the writing workshop. *How's It Done: Teachers' Planning Books* allows you to look into the plan books of two teachers who organize the writing workshop a bit differently.

You might wonder why teachers often engage students in the writing workshop for only a portion of class time in a week or month. The writing workshop will improve student writing as represented on many different measures, high-stakes tests among them. The process of collaboration that is characteristic of the writing workshop will improve student understanding of how to write, but it isn't useful in all situations. During ACT tests, students will not be allowed to ask peers to give them feedback on their writing. We must give them practice in this kind of writing, because it holds an important position in higher education and in many work situations. Again, the skills learned in the writing workshop—deliberate and thoughtful planning, effortful prewriting, revision, editing, audience awareness—should greatly and positively influence the way that students operate in all writing contexts, but students must have practice using them in compressed situations. The writing workshop slows down the writing process, helps novice writers to understand all that goes in to productive writing, and continues to help even skillful writers by providing a community, an audience, and a workspace. It shouldn't be thought of as a minor league that one graduates out of. It should be thought of as a crucial element of learning to write.

## Materials Needed for the Writing Workshop

Teachers eager to implement the writing workshop often ask, "What do I need?" They are accustomed to a new curriculum coming with professionally published materials. One of the advantages of the writing workshop is that it needs no predeveloped materials that have to be purchased from a publisher. There is no need for student textbooks or workbooks. What students do need is some version of a writer's notebook, where they can journal, keep notes, and sometimes begin first drafts; one file to keep work in progress; and one file to keep work that they consider finished. Before beginning your work in the writing workshop, you will want to gather together those important materials.

Teachers who elect to have students draft on computers, and I encourage that if at all possible, will need to have students bring a flash drive if they are unable, or you do not want them to, save work to a school or district network or other repository. It is worth looking into

## How's It Done?: Teachers' Planning Books

Mr. S spends 2 days per week doing writing workshop and 3 days per week working on writing that he considers more teacher directed. While Monday and Tuesday are workshop days, Wednesday, Thursday, and Friday resemble a more traditional composition class. Mr. S has students working on a big paper during the writing workshop and smaller pieces that he explicitly instructs during the end-of-the-week activities. Ms. B elects to do the writing workshop every day for a period of weeks and then focus an entire week on another genre of writing that isn't what she calls "workshoppable." Here are their plan books.

**Mr. S's Plans**

| Monday | Tuesday | Wednesday | Thursday | Friday |
|---|---|---|---|---|
| Writing workshop | Writing workshop | Timed writing | Work with thesis writing | Work with thesis writing |

**Ms. B's Plans**

| Monday | Tuesday | Wednesday | Thursday | Friday |
|---|---|---|---|---|
| Writing workshop | Writing workshop | Writing workshop | Writing workshop | Writing workshop |
| Same | Same | Same | Same | Same |
| Same | Same | Same | Same | Same |
| Test-taking writing | Test-taking writing | Test-taking writing | Test-taking writing | Test-taking writing |

tools such as Google Docs (*documents.google.com*) if you wish students to save their work in a Web-based environment. With free tools such as this one, students can post drafts that can be accessed by themselves, by you, or by other students (by invitation). Their work is not accessible to anyone except the "collaborators" whom the writers invite to view their work. This can be an effective tool not just for storage but also for peer feedback. Using technologies such as this one to support group and teacher feedback on student writing is discussed in Chapters 7 and 8.

# CHAPTER THREE

# Writing Assignments

## Ready to Begin

It's day 1 of your writing workshop, and you've carefully planned the appropriate structures and processes that you'll use to help your students become collaborative members of a productive writing community. You've completed a physical arrangement of your classroom to accommodate students as they move through each step of the writing process. You've explained and modeled the most important aspects of the process. You've acknowledged to your students that they will continue to learn the process throughout the first weeks of writing workshop.

Now it's time to give your first writing assignment. You may want to consider choosing a genre for your first go-around that is comfortable for novice writers, enabling students to focus on their writing as they simultaneously become accustomed to working in the context of workshop processes. This will also help you as you learn how to manage students, subject, and space. In addition, starting with an enjoyable writing task will allow students to begin building positive associations with writing and scaffold their ability to respond to one another.

There remains the question of what kinds of writing assignments are the most gentle and intuitive and the most palatable for teachers and students alike. Remember that this initial period is as much about teaching the practices as it is about anything else, so diving into a difficult literary analysis is probably unwise. Later in this chapter we will talk about the role of student choice in the writing workshop, and this is a good option for the initial days. That is, allow students to select what they wish to write about. You might determine, however, that more direction at the beginning serves your students well, as too much choice can be overwhelming.

Certainly the best writing classrooms offer students and teachers a range of writing experiences. Some students thrive in writing fiction; others are more comfortable in poetry or essay form. Although fiction is often perceived as the most creative, anyone who reads Joan Didion (see *Marrying Absurd*) or Richard Rodriguez (see *Going Home Again: The New American Scholarship Boy*) knows that essay writing can be just as innovative and engaging as fiction. Assignments that demand freshness come in all packages.

Essay writing is a privileged form of discourse in many academic circles. It is valued in the academy as a logical way to present information. Although it is among the genres that we teach students, it does not hold a higher priority than other genres in the writing workshop. In fact we may teach students that there are many kinds of assignments that can be logically structured as five-paragraph essay or not. In the real world, the content of writing helps shape its form. Students who really have something to say rarely need to get those words to fit into a predefined structure to make their point clearly. The difficulty for novice writers is figuring out what needs saying—a challenge that is addressed in Chapter 4 in a discussion of coming up with ideas to write about. In this chapter I begin by talking about what some would consider the iconic assignment in process writing: the personal narrative. While elementary school teachers have great comfort with this genre, it has often been misunderstood in the higher grades.

## The Advantages of Personal Narratives for Initial Assignments

Narrative writing has great reasons to recommend it when teaching students how to work the writing process. In order for students to maximally benefit from peer feedback, the topics must be engaging to their peers and to themselves. Nothing is more engaging to students than their own stories. Furthermore, this allows students to write about something that they know more about than anyone else in the room—you included. What a refreshing change for students who almost never feel that they can inform the teacher about anything. It is probably also true that these topics won't always be particularly engaging to you. If you are an experienced teacher and have read more texts about teenage summer vacations than you care to recall, you might listen to Jessica Siegal, a former high school English teacher who makes a compelling argument for the benefits of personal writing. When interviewed by Samuel Freedman (1991) in a book on the difficulties of teaching in an urban high school he noted:

> Jessica depends on youthful vanity and self-absorption. They are her allies in encouraging her students to write, "Presumably it's a subject they care about—their lives." Jessica once said in explaining her emphasis on autobiographies. "It's not what I did on my summer vacation or what I think about capital punishment. I'm asking them for their feelings, their thoughts. Which may be powerful enough to break down the writing blocks. I mean, how is someone who was in a car accident going to learn to walk again? Not by sitting in a chair. By trying out muscles. However painful that is at first. So the next time, it doesn't hurt as much." (pp. 45–46)

Ms. Siegal centers her writing instruction on her students' lives and believes that by doing so they explore both their writing and themselves. The American poet Richard Hugo concurs: "A writing course may be one of the last places you can go where your life still matters." Far from being childish or trite, personal narrative can have great power and offer opportunity for learning writing and learning about oneself.

Teachers who engage students in the writing process have a wide range of views on the kinds of assignments that are most successful even within the genre of personal narrative. These range from extremely prescriptive to fully student chosen and everything in between. But you will be hard pressed to find a teacher who doesn't value the writing students do about their own unique experiences. Students should be allowed to select the stories that they are interested in sharing. It is difficult for students to engage meaningfully in writing on a topic that is required of them rather than a topic that they have selected. The stories of our lives are essential to the way we communicate, from childhood through adolescence and into adulthood. Jim Trelease (2001), an author and literacy educator, believes "story is the vehicle we use to make sense of our lives in a world that often defies logic" (p. 37). Again, allowing student choice in their writing is essential.

## Thinking about Content, Form, and Topic

Given that all students will write about themselves, you may wonder whether there is any room for assignments. It is not necessarily the case that students should always be free to write about any content. If you never introduce students to various forms of writing, they may never happen upon them by themselves. If you never give them a topic, they may be limited by their own understanding of what is textworthy. Allowing students to write about themselves does not mean that they will write about anything and everything in any way they like. You might find it helpful to distinguish between writing content, writing forms, and writing topics when you think about helping students learn about writing while allowing them to control their own work. "Topic" refers to the assignment parameters. You might ask all students, for instance, to write a quick introduction to themselves. When you do this, the "introduction of myself" is the students' topic. "Form" is the structure in which you ask them to present their writing and is closely related to genre. Are you asking them to write this as a list of elements about themselves? In paragraph form? As a comparison to someone else? Many students are helped by these kinds of limits. In this case you will have delineated the form of the writing and the topic of the writing. What you have not done is choose their content. Students are free to present themselves in any way they wish. The story or list of characteristics that they select is their content. An example of topic, form, and content for two students is shown in Figure 3.1. You will note that Bethanny was responding to a topic given to her by her teachers and that Travis came up with his own topic. All assignments give students some choice in what they want to write, but personal writing of this sort is open-ended in a way that more academic forms often are not. You may wish to begin the writing workshop with assignments that are open for student-selected content but are structured with parameters for topic and form. Consider the three assignments used in a writing workshop in a rural high school shown in Figure 3.2.

   Although all of these assignments are very open-ended in the content the students might select, they are also quite prescriptive in their organization. Note that each one of them breaks the task into compo-

| Student | Topic | Form | Content |
|---------|-------|------|---------|
| Bethanny | Teacher assigned: Talk about a time when you did something you thought was ordinary but turned out to be momentous. | Personal narrative | The swim meet where I came in the middle of the pack every race. |
| Travis | Self-selected: Tell about my favorite coach. | Personal narrative Argument | Coach Roland was the best coach. I am going to write about the one day that he taught me the most and show why this kind of coaching is best for me. |

**FIGURE 3.1.** Topic, form, content.

nent parts for the student writer. Far from dictating the way the text will sound, this simply dictates the elements to consider. Students who need less structure in their writing because they have internalized various patterns of organization can be encouraged to depart from this structure (perhaps after a first draft). Students who need even more support for encoding their ideas in a meaningful pattern for a reader can be offered a graphic organizer or planner (see discussion of prewriting in Chapter 4) to help them visualize the flow of the paper. Assignments like those described above (and more that appear at the end of this chapter) are successful because they push students to reflect on their experiences as meaningful and help them present this meaning in coherent fashion.

## The Boundaries of Personal Narratives

Certainly it would be just as easy to offer a structure for a piece of writing focused on literary analysis or secondary research. Those kinds of writing experiences are crucial for high school students to succeed in upper-level courses and into their college coursework. However it is difficult to teach students to use the writing process if they do not write about what they know intimately, at least initially. Like many high school teachers, you may be concerned about the content that students

Discuss a characteristic that you admire in others but feel you don't have in yourself. Be sure to (1) show the characteristic of a person in action (don't tell what it is, show it); (2) say why you admire the characteristic; (3) give an example from your life where you show your limitations in this area; (4) say why you would like to act in different ways; and (5) discuss steps you might take to acquire these characteristics.

Talk about a time when your experiences of an event violated your expectations of that event. First tell about your expectations, including why you expected it to be that way. Then tell what actually happened. Finally, talk about why you think there was a difference in what you predicted would happen and the reality of the actual event.

Many, many people have influenced us all in our lives. Just about everything about us—the way we talk, dress, think, believe—has been influenced by parents, peers, or friends. It is easy to see how people this close to us affect our lives. It is also interesting to think about how our lives have been altered by people we didn't know well. We have all been affected by strangers or by people we barely know. In this paper, depart from discussing people we would expect to influence your life to explore some of the more surprising ones. Perhaps it is a person whom you knew for a very short time, who walked into and out of your life but you've never forgotten; a person you have never met but have observed closely in a class, on the street, in an airplane; or a person you have never met or seen but have come to know through the media. Be sure to do the following: (1) show you "before"—what were you doing prior to this encounter or series of encounters?; (2) describe the person and the circumstances by which you came to know him or her; (3) show specifically how this person has influenced you—what he or she did and why it touched you; and, finally, (4) give evidence of your change—what are you doing now that is different?

**FIGURE 3.2.** Sample writing assignments. Based on Willey and Berne (1997).

will write when given such free reign. There are wide ranges of topics that adolescence might select that don't fit well in the context of school.

You might discuss with students the difference between personal writing and private writing. Many students might relish the opportunity to reveal pieces of their lives to their peers and their teacher, but others are content to write about less personal events. A writing classroom is not a therapy session, and you will want to be clear that telling deep, dark secrets is not required or necessarily encouraged. There are also topics that are not appropriately shared because they violate school codes of conduct related to profanity, diversity, or bullying. Again, this should be a discussion you have with your students and can fall under the writing skill of attention to audience. When the audience is a school audience, the norms may be different than if the audience is a friend or family member.

Whatever content students choose, it is incumbent on them as writers to let the reader into their experiences. The greatest power in the writing workshop comes from students with a legitimate claim to the term *author*—that is, with the ultimate authority over their paper. Students who know more about what they are writing about than anyone else in the room—the teacher included—engage in an authentic writing experience that more "school-like" experiences cannot replicate. In addition, as is discussed in Chapter 7, engaging in peer response groups is a crucial component of the writing process. These groups function optimally when the group is engaged in the writer's piece, quite a natural state when the writer is sharing a story of his or her own life. It is much more difficult to teach students to give quality feedback on more academic kinds of writing. Teaching students to give and receive the right kind of constructive feedback on all genres of writing starts with teaching them to respond to each other's personal stories.

Many teachers who believe in the power of personal narrative also value teaching students other genres, and they do so during the writing workshop. Expository and argumentative writing can also be generated through a personal tie. Students might begin an academic argument by presenting a situation that interested them, a situation that can be framed as a story from their lives and can meaningfully anchor a more generally informative piece of writing.

In addition to topics with structures like the ones described in this chapter, many writing process advocates note the importance of student choice not only of content but also of topic and genre. You will probably want to offer at least some opportunities for students to search their own interests for writing that appeals to them for any number of reasons. This is also a productive way for students to use techniques for selecting and narrowing topics, activities that help them prepare to write for all kinds of audiences and purposes.

## Suggested Methods for Managing Variation in Pace

One of the hallmarks of writing process classrooms is that students work at their own pace. Because writers frequently draft, get feedback, and revise in different manners, even students who all work with the same intensity will finish at different times. For instance one student might do a good deal of revision between first and second drafts so that their paper is ready for submission to you and consequent publication after that second draft. Another student might make fewer changes between drafts one and two, then make more significant ones between two and four. That student will be on a different pace than the first, yet both are engaging in the writing process by practicing skills and strategies, and both may write an equal amount. More discussion of this follows in subsequent chapters, but the notion of flexibility in student pace is important when thinking about writing assignments and when students can be expected to be ready for a new assignment.

Nobody wants part of the class sitting still while they wait for their peers to finish. Yet it can be rather chaotic to have students beginning new papers while others are still working. Teachers who are newer to writing process instruction often begin by taking the class through the first several assignments in unison. That is, they allow students to work at varying paces but "hold up" the students who move through their writing faster by creating work for them that is outside the activities of writing process instruction so that the entire class can begin the next assignment together.

For example if John is done with his paper on Wednesday, yet many students will be writing for the next several days, he might be assigned to do some independent reading and pay particular attention to author's craft. Another idea would be to ask John to do some informal journal writing that can be mined for future writing topics. If students do not have work waiting for them after completing their writing, they may want to rush through and neglect real writing work. If students are allowed to work independently on other homework or general independent reading once they have finished, they may decide to work more quickly, not create that additional draft, or not edit as carefully as they could. Thus you may want to manufacture a worthwhile task that is difficult and can create a disincentive for moving too quickly. We sometimes refer to these as holding pattern activities. See *How's It Done?: Holding Pattern Activities* for an example of a list of such activities created by an 11th-grade teacher. This teacher expected that students would look through the list she generated when they were waiting for other students to finish. These activities would be submitted along with their drafts as evidence of all the work they did during the writing workshop. No matter that this work did not contribute to the finished paper, it very much contributed to the dynamics of the

## How's It Done?: Holding Pattern Activities

If you are finished with a draft and are awaiting an opportunity to conference, or if you are finished and have submitted your final draft, please select one of the following activities. You'll need to mark these in your log and place them in your final portfolio of writing. Don't be concerned if you don't finish. You can always return to it next time you are in a holding pattern.

■ Come up with ideas in your writing journal of things you want to draft about during the next free-choice assignment. This should be done on loose paper so you can turn it in. You'll still be able to refer to it whenever you want; just go to your portfolio and look.

■ Write a letter to the next group of students whom I have, telling them about one of the important processes in the writing workshop: peer feedback pitfalls, editing tips, planning strategies, revision reminders. Help them understand how we operate and why.

■ Write about something that you don't want to share with the class or me. If you fold it up and write "Private" on it, I'll mark off that you did it, but I won't read it.

■ Look through our classroom library to find a really good example of an author writing with voice. Remember that a text with voice will have a distinct sound. Write down a short passage and tell where it is from and why you think it is a good model. (You can do the same with organization, word choice, sentence fluency, imagery, or detail).

classroom. Students who finish will be disruptive to others unless they are meaningfully occupied.

As will be discussed in later chapters, there are places within the writing process (e.g., the drafting stage; see Chapter 4) when it is advantageous to move quickly. Generally, though, research shows that excellent writers take time to get feedback, consider feedback, and respond to that feedback.

It often happens that a student is done with a draft but must wait for feedback because the teacher or other students are not ready. Part of the management of the writing workshop is creating a system wherein the students are responsible for logging the activities of the day so you can track where they are in their assignments and whether that is a reasonable place for that student to be.

Figure 3.3 shows the writing workshop activity report for 1 week for a student named Mia. There are several things to note about Mia's log. First she is responsible for noting the activities that she participated in on each day. If there are multiple activities, as on Tuesday, she notes how long the first one took so her teacher has a good feel for how much time she is spending on various components. Second, on Thursday, Mia is ready for a conference with her teacher to discuss her third draft, yet the teacher is not ready for her. She has been given the same kinds of choices that John had when he finished his writing before many of his classmates did. Activities like journal writing support writing achievement and are simple enough to be done without instruction once they are explained at the beginning of the year. When

| Date:<br>Name:<br>Mia R | Monday<br>3/11 | Tuesday<br>3/12 | Wednesday<br>3/13 | Thursday<br>3/14 | Friday<br>3/15 | Teacher<br>feedback |
|---|---|---|---|---|---|---|
| **This is what I did:** | Peer group | Peer group finishing (9:30) Revising based on peer feedback | Still revising | Waiting for teacher conference Journal writing | Teacher conference Revising | |
| **Draft:** | 2 | 2 | 2→3 | 3 | 3 | |

**FIGURE 3.3.** Model weekly schedule for Mia.

Mia turns in this paper for final evaluation, she will have to include evidence of any other work she did while waiting for a group to form for peer feedback, while waiting for the teacher (as she did on Thursday) or while waiting for other students to complete a paper she has already completed. There are times when students are ready for others (the teacher or other students) and must learn to be patient. Mia's teacher looks at student logs at the end of the week, initialing them so that she can keep track of her students and so she can note any significant problems that can be identified through student activity reports. Other teachers ask students to submit reports of this kind only when they are ready to submit a paper for evaluation. They use this checkpoint as the place to give credit for appropriately moving through the writing process.

## Helping Students Self-Pace with New Assignments

You may prefer to allow students to move along with their next piece of writing rather than place them in a "holding pattern" as they wait for fellow students to complete the work. It may be less important to you to keep students together than to keep the energy for writing moving along. Since you will nearly always be engaged in conferencing with students about their writing (discussed in Chapter 8) during the writing workshop, you are generally unavailable to assign a new paper or to help a student begin to decide what to write about next. Students need to learn what to do to move independently to the next task.

One urban high school teacher has a large binder with multiple pockets. In each pocket are copies of potential assignments that students can browse when they are ready to begin. They then "sign out" an assignment by taking a copy and leaving a blank sheet with their name and the date on it in its place. This way other students who might want to work on a common assignment know who is doing what and the teacher has a record of who is doing what. Another teacher in that school keeps a database of possible assignments on a computer and students merely look and select one. These techniques work for teachers who give assignments and also for teachers who always or sometimes allow students choice. If you wish students to mix personal choice and teacher-directed writing, you might instruct students to go to the "free-choice" section of a binder and, once they have determined a topic, place a paper with that topic in the section. This helps keep you apprised of student plans and may help generate writing ideas for other students. These can be very simple (e.g., "I am writing about the difficulty of making a decision about going out for the track team") or much more elaborate (e.g., "My plans are to write an account of my first car accident. I am going to try to write it from the perspective of me, my passenger, and maybe the person in the other car. I'll see what happens"), based upon your preference. In either event, the teacher can leave a model in the notebook that students can refer to when they are filing their free-choice plan. Students should know what percentage of their writing can be free choice, if any writing assignments over a span of time must be free choice, what choices are not appropriate, and any other details related to this activity. The next chapter discusses planning. Part of planning is the activity of selecting a topic and whether topics are self-selected, teacher generated, assigned or not assigned; this cues the writing process.

One experienced writing workshop teacher created a number of assignments designed to give students the opportunity to tell their stories, but with a prompt that may offer guidance or structure. This example is shown in *How's It Done?: One Teacher's Assignments*. They may be useful when building an assignment notebook for students or for assigning a whole class to write on the same topic. These, together with the assignments described earlier in the chapter, will give a solid start for many teachers who can then come up with adaptations, omissions, or replacements.

## The Writing Workshop and High-Stakes Tests

High-stakes writing tests are a specialized genre of writing that are important in any writing course. Many teachers give students timed prompts to practice the skill of writing with the clock ticking. Although this isn't really what the writing workshop is all about, skilled students will have practiced internalizing strategies for feedback and revision that will translate to prompted, timed tasks. The writing workshop is especially helpful to students in strategically approaching high-stakes test writing because it allows them to mimic a version of a writing process in more truncated form. For example once students have spent time learning to plan, draft, revise, and edit, you might give them

## How's It Done?: One Teacher's Assignments

Come up with two times in your life that seem very different but in which you acted the same way. One might be an early childhood memory and one from more recently. When you think about both of them, although what happened may be very different, you'll want to say, "Yep, that is me."

Adages are all around us and are common in many different cultures. Sometimes adages help make sense of the world and sometimes they confuse us further (for instance, does absence make the heart grow fonder or is the person out of sight, out of mind.) For this assignment, please come up with an adage that is common in your culture and show an example of how it might be untrue for you; that is, disprove its legitimacy in at least one instance.

Talk about a possession that is important to you but that has little monetary or external value. This may be something that was given to you by someone special; it may be something that you associate with a significant time in your life; it may be something you love for no clear reason. First describe what it is. Then tell the story of how it came to gain such prestige in your life. Finally, tell why and how it has endured for you even when other things that may have cost more or been more aesthetic or useful have fallen away. You may also wish to include a description of the response of others to your object.

Discuss a time when an authority figure (a parent, coach, teacher, clergy, or the like) gave you bad advice. What were the circumstances? Did you take it? What were the results? Why do you think they were "wrong"?

Peer pressure is a fact of life for children and adults. Sometimes succumbing to it goes against our better interests. Other times it can be a productive way to make better choices than we might make on our own. Certainly in a behavior like smoking, there will be instances of groups that helped people avoid it and instances of groups that seem to promote it. For this paper, think of a time when you were a part of a group that helped convince someone else to do something. Looking back, are you glad you were a part of that group?

**Exercise 1:** Ask students to divide the time they have to write in fourths. If, for instance, they have 40 minutes to complete a task, they might practice spending 5 minutes planning, 20 minutes drafting, 10 minutes rereading and revising, and 5 minutes editing. After reflecting on this time breakdown, students try again with other time allotments.

**Exercise 2:** Students might read one another's practice prompts and give feedback to show each other how to think about giving feedback to oneself.

**FIGURE 3.4.** Timed writing practice.

experiences with test-preparatory exercises like the versions shown in Figure 3.4.

You will do students a world of good if they have enough experiences getting feedback from a reader so that they are able to internalize feedback as a necessary part of challenging writing. Once this notion is solid, modeling and practicing prompting revision on a student's own work will be of great assistance on any timed writing task.

CHAPTER FOUR

# Planning and Prewriting

## The Role of Prewriting in the Writing Process

Getting started with a writing assignment—no matter whether the topic is assigned or chosen by the writer—can be the most challenging part of the task for novices. It can also be challenging for teachers who want the writer's experience to be positive, energizing, and constructive.

We know that good writers engage in significant prewriting and/or planning before they write. We also know that this process is not uniform across writers or, even for a single writer, across writing tasks. In addition, it is not true that there is a right or wrong or good or bad way to begin to write. Ralph Fletcher (2000) believes, "Here's the bottom line: Whatever prewriting you do should build your energy to write, not deflate that energy. I've known too many writers who devote so much time and energy to their prewriting that they are absolutely sick of the topic before they even start writing it!" He warns, "Beware of prewriting the life out of your topic" (p. 30). You will want to share with student writers the range of techniques available to them as they struggle to begin writing. You may also want them to practice doing some of them to see which work the best, but you likely won't prescribe the method they use when they begin to engage in writing that is meaningful to them. No prewriting activity is useful if it doesn't lead

41

quickly to writing, and so it is unproductive to demand that all students use the same strategies. Filling out a graphic organizer, brainstorming a long list of possible topics, or talking with friends about plans for a paper can all be helpful forms of prewriting, but they are not ends in themselves. The goal is writing.

Although common models of the writing process list a single event—"prewriting" (sometimes called invention, sometimes called planning)—there are really two different, sometimes intersecting, parts of preparing to write. *Prewriting* is the process by which students come up with an idea of where to start. Fletcher and Portalupi (2001) says, ["although] the term sounds formal and intimidating . . . [just as] athletes warm up by stretching muscles, every writer has his or her own way of warming up to the task of writing" (p. 63). *Planning* is taking an idea that has already been selected (either by the student or by the teacher or a standardized test creator) and thinking through how to cope with it in written form. The difference between *prewriting* and *planning* is pertinent. Sometimes students are given a directive topic and need not "invent" it, yet they will likely need to do significant planning to think through an approach to it. Many times, students will prewrite to come up with or narrow an idea and then plan how to present the idea. They are engaging, then, in a two-part process as depicted in Figure 4.1. Some students spend much time deciding on topics and ultimately plan very little. Some do both every time; a few might do neither. The task often dictates the manner in which students begin. Less difficult writing tasks may demand less explicit planning. More restricted topics may demand less prewriting. You will want to be certain to offer a range of strategies for both activities as well as

---

**Prewriting**
- Done to come up with an idea.
- Can be done orally, in written form, or internally.
- May be assisted by prewriting techniques like free-writing and brainstorming.

**Planning**
- Done once an idea is at least partially formed.
- Can be done orally, in written form, or internally.
- May be assisted by planning mnemonic or other strategy.

---

**FIGURE 4.1.** Prewriting versus planning.

discuss the distinctions, always with Fletcher's caveat—the goal is to move through this process so that a writer writes. Over time students will find what works for them or find that different strategies work on different days or for different tasks. Strategies for prewriting and planning are discussed separately in the following sections.

## Getting Your Students Started through Prewriting

As part of a piece of a mini-lesson (or series of mini-lessons) on prewriting, you might ask students to come up with a list of ideas for a paper recommending an improvement to their school. Once that list is generated (a variety of strategies for generation are discussed below), students share their ideas and ask for peer feedback on which one sounds most interesting. You could do this as a whole-group activity, leading the class in considerations of topics, or have students work in small groups or pairs. Although the writer is not obligated to select the "most popular" among the peers, he or she does get an inkling of audience interest in the forthcoming text. The peers will be the audience, at least initially, and it may help to know what topic they will engage with most.

The student is best served in activities like this if he or she has many ideas. It is important for novice writers to have as many choices as possible in case one text falls flat. Sophomore writing student Jorie might have three ideas for changes she wishes high school administrators would include in the school improvement plan: Start later in the day, have laptops available for student use during classes, and improve the quality of the cafeteria food. In her group or with the assistance of the whole class and her teacher, she might learn which of these issues is most pressing for other students, and this may influence her to go with that idea. She also might ask peers to help her come up with some reasons for each and decide to write the one that has the most support. She is also free to go with the one she likes best even if that wasn't the one favored by others. Authors have *author*ity over their own texts in the writing workshop just as they do in real life. Although the writer might seek advice, he or she should feel obligated only to carefully consider what someone else says. This kind of decision making involves analytic skill and creative thought, higher-order thinking skills that you will want to encourage. By the time Jorie or another writer sits down to write, they have made many important and sometimes challenging decisions. They may have accepted and/or rejected a number of ideas based on information that is analyzed and put into action. This analytic process is one reason why you may elect to give students at least some choice in their topic selection. There are certainly other reasons related to motivation and engagement (look back at Chapter 2 for a fuller discussion of assignments and topics) to give students freedom to select—yet even without these, picking is in itself educative. It is true that standardized tests can be extremely directive to students, thus taking away these decision-making activities; however, students skilled in thinking of writing as series of processes and plans will be better prepared to tackle a variety of writing tasks. Edgar Schuster, a former high school English teacher (and author (2003) of *Breaking the Rules: Liberating Writers through Innovative Grammar Instruction*), writes in a 2004 article: "I once spent 40 minutes prewriting an essay on a test timed for an hour. On another occasion, I plunged right in: My essay itself was essentially a prewrite—and not a very good one" (p. 376). His description of his own process reminds us all that nothing about the writing process is uniform. Nonetheless, both were strategies that he strove to employ. Helping students practice what to do when faced with more or less open-ended tasks increases their chances of approaching the tasks with some measure of confidence.

## Methods to Help Students Generate Ideas through Prewriting

Students will and should customize the writing process to suit their own style and preferences. In a writing course, however, introducing students to various options helps expand their repertoire. Not all students will like, benefit from, or tolerate the activities below. In the interest of true understanding of the activities, though, you'll want to introduce the strategies, model them, and then help students to practice. After a few practice sessions, you might suggest to students that they pick one of these strategies to use on their next prewriting task.

### Free-Writing

Free-writing can be both enjoyable and productive for spurring lots of other writing. Writers, especially struggling writers, are often discouraged about the quality of their writing even before they put anything on paper. This attitude keeps them from the fluid, almost unconscious act of putting words on paper that is so important to many writing tasks. Writers often write to find out what they think, not just to tran-scribe what they know they think. Yet the lucidity necessary to write unencumbered by internal monitors is not natural for many writers. Because free-writing requires that students write without monitoring their thoughts, without doubting themselves, they are "free" (hence the name) to explore words, phrases, and ideas that they might never access in a more constrained context. Free-writing is ungraded, some-times unshared, often tossed aside, but sometimes invaluable in figur-ing out what the writer knows. In a free write, students are asked to write uninterrupted for a period of time. This period of time should be rather short initially (maybe 5 minutes) and can gradually increase over time as students become more comfortable. Students put pen to paper or finger to keyboard and write with as little monitoring as pos-sible. As students are learning to free-write, you will want to ask them to keep their writing going at any cost. If a student is stuck, he or she can write the last word repeatedly until new words come. Free-writing done in preparation for a particular assignment or writing task might start with some focus—maybe a word or two at the top of a page—or it may be entirely open. Following the free-write, students take a min-ute, then read their writing. If they are surprised at what they said, they have really mastered this technique. Sometimes they find what Fletcher (1996) calls a "seed" of an idea that they may want to pursue. Other times they find nothing worth pursuing and move on to another free write or another prewriting technique. With practice, free-writing becomes more and more natural for students. Many teachers join their students in this practice in preparation for their own writing.

Free-writing in preparation to write a more finished piece does not end with the putting down of pens or hitting save on the keyboard. Students will likely need significant scaffolding to see this kind of writ-ing as generative. Part of your teaching will be helping them to mine this writing for kernels that have promise. After an early free-write, you will want to help students learn to lay aside their writing, perhaps engage briefly in another task, and then return to it with fresh eyes. Help them analyze their own free-writing without preconceptions about what it does or does not have.

## Brainstorming

Brainstorming is like free-writing: The goal is to take away the barriers that keep people from thinking creatively. This technique, borrowed from paneled boardrooms where business executives tried to invent new products and services and were encouraged to say whatever came to mind, no matter how ridiculous, relies on either verbal or written lists of components. Tompkins (2004) describes brainstorming in this way: "Students generate a list of words or ideas on a topic . . . they think about the topic and then list as many examples, descriptors, or characteristics as possible. Afterward, students circle the most promising ideas to use in a writing activity" (p. 215).

Juniors beginning a paper on responsibilities and rights generated the following list of topics while brainstorming ideas:

- Money
- Freedom
- Transportation
- Family
- Speeding

- With money come rights
- Age
- Education
- Friendships

- Wearing seatbelts
- Parents
- Freeloading
- Voting
- The Constitution

Their teacher recorded their responses on the whiteboard and asked students to select a few to put on paper in front of them. From the larger list, then, they narrowed and added if they elected to do so. Like free-writing, brainstorming sometimes yields great ideas and sometimes does not. Students should be required to engage in these kinds of activities to get experience doing so and then use them when they find themselves making the writerly decision to do so.

### Imaging

Prewriting does not always involve words. Images can also spur thinking. You can model for students how pictures can spur thought. Put a large piece of chart paper on the board and begin to doodle, draw, web—whatever comes. Visual learners may feel comfortable thinking on paper with images rather than words. Imaging can be done like free-writing—very fast—or more slowly.

### Talking

We are wired as a species to tell stories; many cultures have rich oral traditions that rely on verbally transferred information. Tapping into that skill can help students to improve both their oral and written literacy skills. Many reluctant writers have significant experience talking their way into and out of schoolwork. This skill can be channeled into a prewriting activity. Some teachers take out small tape players and ask students who like to talk more than they like to write to speak into them. Students can then replay the recording and try to note the good ideas that were once verbally fleeting. Small children who don't have letter-forming or encoding skills often speak their stories into a tape recorder or to an adult who transcribes their words. This is constructing meaning in much the same way that writers do and can be used as a transition to more conventional writing.

## Writer's Notebooks

One writerly quality is the ability to look around, to notice, to inspect. Writer's notebooks are both places for recording these inspections and tools to encourage the activity. They can be used as journals, as observation tools, or as a combination of many kinds of writing. Some teachers require students to keep writer's notebooks, and others suggest this as an ongoing prewriting activity. Ralph Fletcher has done fine work on the role of the writer's notebook in the development of student writing. See his book *What a Writer Needs* (1993) for an in-depth discussion of writer's notebooks.

## Using Technology

Although writing is generally a low-resource subject, there are products on the market that can assist students in many aspects of the writing process, prewriting included. Programs like Inspiration or Kidspiration (Helfgott & Westhaver, 2006a, 2006b) help students by showing them ways to organize random ideas. These programs ask students to enter words and then help manipulate them to reveal connections or extensions of thoughts. In addition, these programs can be useful for you to examine (many have 30-day free trials) even if you don't order them because they can prompt some of these organizing techniques that can be used without the assistance of the computer. For instance Inspiration allows students to select various-sized and -shaped icons and shows them many ways to manipulate those icons to consider relationships and organizational patterns. This can also be done on paper, without the assistance of a computer. Other programs (e.g., Writer's Helper) help by asking questions about a topic. If the student submits the word "freedom," for example, the computer prompts questions about the subject. Again, if students don't have continuous access to computer programs like this one, they can still learn questioning as a technique for seeing ideas in new and complex ways.

Current Internet technology can also play a significant role in help-ing students decide what to write about. Bloggers regularly post ideas that beg for responses. Responding to a real person, even one who can-not be seen, has innumerable benefits for student reading, writing, and thinking. In addition, blogs, like all kinds of reading, can spur ideas that can begin new writing. Online chats can do the same thing. One level of participation may be a student interacting with others about the topic. Another might be the student using something said to begin a new piece that can be worked on in writing workshop. There are cer-tainly security concerns related to these kinds of activities in schools, but school media specialists and instructional technologists can help you to limit access to online environments to those that are education-ally appropriate.

## Strategic Planning as Part of Prewriting

The difference between skills and strategies is that skills are automatic and strategies are intentionally activated. For example when a reader engages with a text that is simple and interesting, he or she likely makes connections as a matter of course. As he or she reads, there are auto-matic tie-ins to personal experience or the world or another text. When that same reader is faced with a far more difficult text, he or she must be intentional about making connections, so that self-talk occurs in order to slow the reader down for this text and activate metacognition (e.g., "Do I understand this?", "What kind of connections might I make to better understand?") Thus a reader might be skillful when confronted with one text and operate strategically on another.

It is the same with writing tasks. There are many kinds of writing that people do effortlessly. They need or want to say something, so they do. When students text message or IM one another, they rarely think carefully about what they are going to say before writing and pressing send. Like the reader who moves easily through a text, any strategies that they might use are invisible and automatic. That is because the cognitive demands of this kind of communication are manageable. We all do a variety of writing tasks with ease. There is no reason to incor-porate explicit planning in these easy, often pleasant writing tasks. When confronted with a less familiar or more demanding writing task, though, writers often slow themselves down to say, "OK, now how do I begin this?" This is approaching the task strategically, slowing it down and activating processes that have been successful in the past. Student writers often have little experience with strategic writing. Like all parts of the writing process, students need discussion, modeling, and guided practice, even in something as simple as asking oneself how to begin. This strategy might seem ineffectual, but it serves an important purpose by stopping students long enough to think.

In a mini-lesson on planning you might bring a writing task that you need to do for your professional life. Maybe it is a grant application, maybe part of a curriculum project or a memo to parents. By placing the "assignment" in front of the students or on the overhead projector or whiteboard, you can think aloud in the following way:

> "OK, I know I have to do this. I see that my audience is the assistant principal and curriculum specialist, so what do I know about how much background information I will have to give them in order for them to understand? I think they know *XYZ*, so I will skip that and just begin writing at the *ABC* point. Now that I have a good sense of my audience, I want to think through my purpose. Am I trying to convince them of something or trying to get them to do what they already said they would do. . ."

By doing this think-aloud, you model the way that writers use previous knowledge of tasks, audience, and purpose to begin to write. Although planning is often implicit, understanding how to do it in an explicit fashion helps students to confidently approach a range of writing tasks.

You can provide scaffolds for students as they learn to do strategic planning. Doug Buehl (2001) recommends RAFT to assist students in writing preparation. This acronym is to remind students to consider the Role, Audience, Format, and Topic for their piece. This can help students to reflect on important writing components prior to writing. You may ask students to write these out so that you can see their thinking, which will help some of them. Others will ultimately elect to do this as a part of their metacognitive processes. See Table 4.1 for a list of planning strategies or, even better, ask students to collaborate with you on ones particular to a writing task, to the nature of the students, or to a whim. The specific strategy is much less important than that students understand the need to have a strategy. It is worth returning to the ideas of skills versus strategies when working with students in these ways. Teachers can remind them that some writing tasks do not require explicit planning—students can start drafting because planning is part of what they are doing without thinking about it, but they need to learn

**TABLE 4.1. Planning Mnemonics**

| Mnemonic | Genre | Stands for . . . | Reference |
|---|---|---|---|
| RAFT | Any | Role, audience, format, topic. | Buehl (2001) |
| STOP | Persuasive | Suspend judgment. Take a side. Organize ideas. Plan more. | De La Paz & Graham (1997) |
| DARE | Persuasive | Develop a topic sentence. Add support. Reject opposition. End with conclusion. | De La Paz & Graham (1997) |
| STOP | Any | Stop and think of purpose. | Troia, Graham, & Harris (1999) |
| LIST | Any | List ideas and sequence them. | Troia, Graham, & Harris (1999) |
| $W^4H^2$ | Story | Who/what/when/where? How does it end? How does character feel? | Graham, Harris, & Mason (2005) |

strategic planning so they can use it when faced with a challenging writing task.

## Sample Mini-Lesson on Planning

Figure 2.2 provides a template for mini-lessons. *How's It Done?: A Mini-Lesson on Planning* is designed to help students think about how to plan their writing. Another mini-lesson focusing on this stage of the writing process might show students how to free-write, brainstorm, or practice another kind of prewriting as discussed above.

## How's It Done?: A Mini-Lesson on Planning

1. **Teacher introduces the portion of the writing process under discussion on this day.**

   "Today we are going to talk about another way of planning your writing. Let's say I have an idea for writing: I have decided I want to write a profile of a student in our class, or perhaps that is an assignment that was given to me by the editor of the school paper. I have the topic, but what else do I need to get started?"

2. **Teacher talks about how students get started in this process.**

   "I know that I am going to select Ross because he has just returned from competing in the state track meet and got the chance to interact with students from all over the state. Instead of going up and asking, 'So how was it?', I think I might want to come up with a plan."

3. **Teacher models the process for the students on chart paper, an overhead, document camera, or the chalkboard.**

   "I am thinking about the kind of piece I want to write because that will dictate the questions I ask. I think I'll focus just on this meet, not on what got him there and not really on the sport. Instead I'll ask him what he noticed about the people on the other teams."

4. **Teacher leads students in practicing the process.**

   "OK, now I am going to give you a topic for writing and ask you to jot down some plans you might use before diving in."

5. **Teacher debriefs the whole group.**

   "What did it feel like to plan in this way? What difficulties did you have? Let's remind ourselves why we might do this on a regular basis."

6. **Teacher prepares students for the physical, cognitive, and social demands of doing this independently.**

   "When you are planning writing on your own, sometimes you will be very strategic about your plans—this is especially true with a more structured writing assignment. Other times you won't go through this kind of process; rather, you will write as part of your planning."

CHAPTER FIVE

# Initial Drafting

## Teaching Students What Drafting Is

It may be easier to help students see what first drafts are not. They are not finished pieces of writing. They are not documents that are evaluated for a grade. They are not end points to be agonized over. They are not pieces of writing that need to be correct.

Because writing process instruction is still in its infancy, it isn't difficult to recall a time when first drafts were something that students submitted to teachers for feedback and sometimes for evaluative marks. Creating the initial text—what we now consider to be one part of the writing process—was once the beginning and ending of writing instruction in school.

I like to explain to students that a first draft is like a pretest. It shows what they are able to do without support and without instruction. When students create first drafts, they are showing their raw writing ability. Some students' initial writing is highly skilled. They may have had lots of experience writing in or out of school. They may be prolific readers who note the author's craft as they read and are able to translate that into their own writing. They may just have a knack for written language. Whatever the reason, they are at a good starting point. However, writers' incoming skills should not be a measure of how much students can grow. Allowing students to continue producing first drafts without pushing them to engage fully in other parts of the writing process to improve their skills is deciding that they need no further instruction. If a math student shows that he or she is able to master material with ease, they are often pushed to higher challenges. We want to push students who write well to further challenges as well. Sometimes this means introducing them to more difficult writing tasks. Sometimes this means asking them to take a competent first draft and really push it to be more.

## Teaching Students to Draft Fearlessly

The iconic advice given to first-draft writers is to think of the activity as very low risk. Donald Murray (1980, p. 5) writes, "The writer drafts a piece of writing to find out what it may have to say . . . each draft must be an exercise in independence as well as *discovery*" (my emphasis). Students often struggle to turn off the monitors that have been embedded in them that suggest that they must decide what they want to write and what the final outcome of their writing will be, before they even put words to page. This kind of writing assumes that students think first, and then write. Many writers believe that, to the contrary, they write to find out what they think. Peter Elbow (1981, p. 7) recommends that writers "first write freely and uncritically so that [they] can generate as many words and ideas as possible without worrying whether they are good; then turn around and adopt a critical frame of mind and thoroughly revise what [they] have written—taking what's good and discarding what isn't and shaping what's left into something strong." The line between free-writing—usually thought of as preparation to write a draft—and drafting isn't always clear, and it doesn't need to be. Some writers think of initial drafting as part of their prewriting. First drafting (sometimes called zero drafting) is about fluency and the ability to sustain writing for a long enough period of time to make enough meaning on a page so that feedback is useful and can be used to create future drafts.

## Making It Easier to Start

Students who experience difficulty writing, or starting their writing, often do so because they are too worried about the end. Freeing students to write first drafts without overfocusing on correctness or craft is the first step toward helping to move them from writing what they know to writing to find out what they know.

A first draft is an investment, not a dividend. It is something you start with, and it can invite its writer to see what happens. If one invests a little and determines it not to yield, they move on—to the next first draft, to another draft of what they just wrote, to a new project entirely. Although this decision isn't always under the control of a student writer in a classroom, it is for real writers. There can be great power in writing for a little while, reading it over, and hitting the delete key. Natalie Goldberg (1986) advises writers to write a lot, to write in notebooks and on scraps of papers, and then to sink into a space and read this writing from afar, the way one might read something written by someone else.

Teaching novice writers to draft with the knowledge that the draft may go nowhere is a challenge. Students who struggle to write, who find it physically, cognitively, or emotionally difficult, are loath to "waste" any writing at all. When we watch a small child labor over a single sentence, we understand that to tell them the sentence is not very good or that it needs to be rewritten demotivates and almost ensures that they will approach the next writing task with trepidation. It isn't so different for adolescents who struggle with writing or simply have never been shown how to write. The page they filled with words likely took significant effort. Smiling and telling them that it is just a first draft and that it can be taken or left will be of little comfort. They did something difficult and they simply prefer not to do it again; that is understandable. The results, however, are often drafts of work that have no life, that contain no interest or energy. You'll want to spend time talking about writing that goes nowhere and about how frustrating but also how useful this can be.

Writing is generative. When one writes, one is able to write more. Time spent writing, even if that writing is eliminated with one strike of the delete key, is not time wasted. Certainly at some point the student must produce something that can be read, but there is lots of time to not do that as well. When golfers go to the driving range, they use their errant drives to learn how to drive better in the future. They don't consider every missed hit wasted activity, because those misses help the athlete improve. Drafting can be like going to the driving range. Sometimes you take a shot and it is beautiful. Other times you look around and hope nobody else noticed. The golfer learns far more from the errors, from thinking through why something sliced, hooked, or never made it very far off the ground, than they do from a perfectly straight 200-yard drive.

An early study of drafting (Glynn, Britton, Muth, & Dogan, 1982) looked at the qualities of first drafts that predict success in final products. The researchers looked at four groups of students: Group 1 did first drafts that contained mostly polished sentences, Group 2 wrote in complete but unpolished sentences, Group 3 used organized notes to start their writing, and Group 4 wrote unorganized notes. This study found that the less structured the initial draft was, the more ideas it contained. If part of the purpose of writing is looking for ideas, the students whose drafts were more polished were less successful. On the structured–unstructured continuum, the group who drafted using only unorganized notes was seen to be the least structured but ended up with the most thoughts. Again, this is a good argument for teaching students to give up control over first drafts and just write them.

## Looking at Elements of Writing

With all that said, we can teach students much about the qualities of a promising first draft. It is a misconception that writing teachers simply tell students to write and wait to see what happens. Instruction in and exposure to various elements of writing helps students to gain knowledge and experience in what good writing is.

This chapter summarizes the most common traits of writing. It is worth noting that many of these overlap, that real writing seldom breaks into neat component parts. Many of these are excellent topics to focus on in beginning-of-workshop mini-lessons. Students benefit from understanding these traits, from discussing successful and unsuccessful examples, and from looking at them in the work of peers and in professional "mentor texts."

Note the sample mini-lessons for each of the traits in the *How's It Done?* box on pp. 59–65.

### *Audience*

Perhaps the greatest gift of writing workshop is that it gives writers an ad hoc audience for their work. Writers can read their work aloud to fellow students or to you, or they can wait close by as others read their work. Writers learn a tremendous amount about their own writing from hearing the responses of others. They are especially poised to learn from this feedback if they are explicitly taught ways to effectively use audience response (discussed in Chapters 7 and 8). Student writers learn that audiences can have different needs (e.g., one student wants to hear more about one part of the story and others think they have heard plenty); they learn, at times, that they are saying more or different things than they had planned; they learn about different perspectives on what they say. These lessons are only possible with the responses of those around them. Students who have audience awareness find that it influences their planning, their drafting, their ways of revising, their editing, and their publishing. It is somewhat like the person who pays no attention to the mess in their car until they have a passenger who has never been in it. Now they see the crumbs and the soda cans on the floor, trash that was there but not really seen until it was considered from the perspective of someone else.

## *Purpose*

Purpose may be the most intangible of all the traits of writing. When students are planning their writing they often consider purpose coupled with a consideration of audience. So they are thinking *for whom* am I writing this and *why*? While the first question may have a tangible answer (e.g., my teacher, other students, legislatures, a publisher), the second can be amorphous. It isn't enough for students to argue that their purpose is to fulfill a writing assignment. While that may well be the case, and that certainly is a purpose, it is not one that is especially helpful in guiding great writing. A well-articulated, authentic purpose helps guide a writer's choices. For example a student may determine that he or she would like to write about an experience on a recent vacation. During planning and drafting, the decisions about what pieces of the vacation to reveal can be circumscribed by the reason for the selection, the purpose for writing. Is it to convince another student to vacation in this location? If so, one would include details about climate, activities, expense, and ease of access. Is the paper intended to tell a funny story that happened on the trip? If so, the details described above might be extraneous and the focus would be on that singular event. Is the purpose to argue for the importance of vacations in general? This would require a very different frame. Student writing is often unfocused. That may mean that the purpose for writing is not entirely clear (at least to the reader). Instruction in the concept of purpose helps students focus their writing and select detail and rhetoric particular to that reason. To help students to learn about purpose, teachers often use the "so what" heuristic. When a purpose isn't entirely clear, you (or peers) may ask, as kindly as possible, "So what?" This phrase serves as a reminder for students that the purpose of the piece needs more clarity. As students develop in their awareness of purpose, this phrase becomes less and less common as a part of the feedback given on their writing. In *How's It Done?: Mini-Lesson on Purpose* notice how one teacher helps her students see the choices that a writer makes when writing with purpose.

## *Voice*

When asked about the difference between a good student paper and a great one, an experienced standardized test rater told me: "Voice." Although students can be organized and coherent in their writing without voice, their writing will probably never shine. Understanding how voice is used can be a continual challenge for student and professional writers, but it is battle worth fighting. You may already have some favorite ways to prompt students' awareness of voice. Any technique that elucidates the difference between texts that do and do not show voice can be effective. One of the most potent lessons on voice may be to ask students to tell a funny story into a tape recorder. Often this verbal example will have inflection, colorful language, and different paces—many of the elements that help distinguish a piece that has voice. It is often much more difficult for students to translate those elements into writing. Sometimes comparing a student's verbal stories with their written ones highlights this very issue. Although I discuss voice, audience, purpose, and word choice separately in this chapter, they are closely related. One often uses voice to convey a purpose. Similarly, one's purpose can determine whether one writes in a more or less lighthearted voice. In *How's It Done?: Mini-Lesson on Voice* one teacher begins the discussion with students on writing with voice. It bears repeating that mini-lessons like the ones described in this chapter and exemplified in the *How's It Done?* boxes are not one-shot deals. A teacher may repeat mini-lessons such as these many times. It is not easy to teach students about the traits of writing, and just because a student successfully writes one piece doesn't mean traits will always come easily. Exposing and reexposing students to the ideas of purpose, voice, and the like will help them approach all sorts of writing tasks with confidence, so teachers should think of this as ongoing instruction.

### Word Choice

The more elements of writing you discuss with students, the more their interrelatedness becomes clear. It is difficult to talk about word choice without touching upon audience awareness, voice, and purpose. Nonetheless, it is important for students to think carefully about how to chose potent and relevant words for the meaning they wish to convey. Students with larger vocabularies are at a great advantage. Shades of meaning can be easily revealed with more precise vocabulary. Vocabularies grow when students read and when they are given explicit instruction in word parts like roots, prefixes, and suffixes. Thus vocabulary instruction should always be considered as a part of instruction in writing, as it significantly increases students' tool kits of available words. At times, doing vocabulary work in the context of writing workshop will help students see how they can expand the range of words they have available to them.

### Organization

Writers organize their work in all sorts of ways. Teaching students about patterns of organization can help them best represent their work to an audience. In writing done outside of writing classrooms, the content and purpose helps to dictate the form. In school, we sometimes ask students to write in varied forms (e.g., cause–effect, comparison–contrast, process analysis, narrative, poetry) so they can have experience doing so. Students should be reminded that when they write in the real world they will have to make choices about how best to organize their writing, and that they should think carefully about their audience needs in doing so. Students can be introduced to narrative and expository structure effectively by explicitly noting those structures as they read.

## Reminding Students about the Place of Drafting

Sometimes students fall in love with their first drafts. When they do so, they may resist changing them. You will want to decide the most reasonable approach given the characteristics of your class or of the one or two students for whom this is an issue. Some teachers decide that one paper per year can be presented as finished without drafts. This would be in response to students who think they have struck the exact chord they want the first time. Although it is quite possible that students do

# How's It Done?: Five Mini-Lessons on Drafting

## MINI-LESSON ON AUDIENCE

1. **Teacher introduces the subject under discussion.**

   "Today we are going to talk about audience. In writing workshop, we benefit greatly from having an audience of other writers to respond to our work. Sometimes the response from the reader is emotional, as we might do if we were sharing final drafts. Other times, peers are listening in order to give advice or feedback on the writing that is being presented. If you listen carefully, you can get lots of insight. If you learn to anticipate what they will say, you may attend to many of their needs before you share with them."

2. **Teacher talks about how students get started in this process.**

   "Often, we will work in peer response groups to get feedback from several people at once. Today we are going to talk about an audience of one—a partner who reads your work and shares impressions, questions, and notes."

3. **Teacher models the process for students on chart paper, an overhead, document camera, or the chalkboard.**

   "Cara was nice enough to read my first draft in order to model this process. She read my first draft and then came up with the following questions and comments. [*Teacher posts text on overhead, document camera, or via LCD projector. After students have read the original text, she puts up the text with Cara's comments on it.*] Now that I have read her comments, I have to think about them. I am thinking that I really agree with this one, so I am going to start there; these other comments are interesting, but I don't think I am going to attend to all of them at once. I will start with this one and go from there."

4. **Teacher leads students in practicing the process.**

   "Now I want you to practice this. Select one brief entry from your writer's notebook and exchange it with a partner. Each student should write two questions or comments on a sticky note and

   *(continued)*

then return it to the writer. Once the writer has the comments back, they must sit and think about which one they might attend to first. Remember, we are going to respect the opinion of our audience, but we don't have to do anything they suggest if, for instance, we can come up with a different change than what was suggested. The important point here is to think hard about what is said."

5. **Teacher debriefs the whole group.**

"OK, someone share a really good piece of advice or question from their partner and tell what it made you think of. Someone else share a piece of advice that you also thought was good but decided not to use. Tell us how you came to that decision."

6. **Teacher prepares students for the physical, cognitive, and social demands of doing this independently.**

"Now when you do this with longer pieces of writing, you may struggle a little. We will continue to practice so that you will improve.

## MINI-LESSON ON PURPOSE

1. **Teacher introduces the subject under discussion.**

"Today we are going to talk about writing with a clearly defined purpose. When we plan and draft, we want to think about why our audience would bother reading our work if they weren't required to because of their participation in a writing class."

2. **Teacher talks about how students get started in this process.**

"Sometimes when the writing task is wide open, the purpose question is the primary one. Let's say I am given free reign to write whatever suits me. I decide that I am going to write about a friend of mine who just published a book. After I read the book, I was put in this awkward position because I didn't really understand it and he asked me my opinion. So that is what I want to write about. As I am writing, I realize that I have to ask: What I am doing? Why am I writing this?"

*(continued)*

3. **Teacher models the process for students on chart paper, an overhead, document camera, or the chalkboard.**

   "Let's say I am partially through the story about reading the book and being completely baffled and I have just written this line, 'There was a moment when I was sure this book made me feel like the stupidest person alive.' Now I am stopping and thinking, that sounds kind of whiny—is my purpose to make myself feel a certain way about my own reading or to discuss the awkwardness of having to discuss the book with my friend? I'll have to think hard about my purpose in order to figure out if that line is really necessary."

4. **Teacher leads student in practicing the process.**

   "Now I want you to take 2 to 3 minutes to write down a description of your bedroom. [*Students are given time to write.*] Now I would like you to imagine that you are writing a description of your bedroom for a specific purpose—to lobby your parents for new carpet or to show why it does not need to be cleaned anytime in the near future." [*Students are given another short time to write.*]

5. **Teacher debriefs the whole group.**

   "What was the difference between writing a neutral description and writing one for a more specific purpose? What words, perspective, or imagery had to change? Please read both versions to a partner to see whether they can hear the differences. See whether they can tell which is which and how they determined it."

6. **Teacher prepares students for the physical, cognitive, and social demands of doing this independently.**

   "When you are drafting your pieces in the next little bit, think about why you are presenting something in a certain way. When you do that you are really thinking about your purpose."

*(continued)*

## MINI-LESSON ON VOICE

1. **Teacher introduces the subject under discussion.**

   "Today we are going to talk about how voice can help enliven your writing. Nobody wants to read work that sounds like a computer wrote it. In fact, the thing I enjoy most about reading your writing is how it sometimes sounds exactly like you. If you think about the texts you really enjoy reading, I think you will realize that they often have very resonant voices."

2. **Teacher talks about how students get started.**

   "When I am writing I think to myself: Am I presenting this as me? Am I thinking about my audience and purpose and adjusting my voice accordingly? What kind of language would be most effective here, and how would it sound?"

3. **Teacher models the process for students on chart paper, an overhead, document camera, or the chalkboard.**

   "I wrote this piece earlier and realize that it is a little dry. I want to add some life to it. What do you think? [*Teacher reads piece of her writing.*] What are some things I might do to add my voice? Now, say I wanted it to sound like someone else wrote it, perhaps my 10-year-old nephew. What would he sound like?"

4. **Teacher leads students in practicing the process.**

   "Now I want you to take a piece of writing from your journal and read it to a partner. [*Students read.*] Now see if you can add something that will help us identify it as yours even if we didn't know who wrote it. Are there some characteristics of your voice that you could translate to paper? After doing that, see if you can make it sound like someone else wrote it—a friend, a celebrity, a parent. What would their voice sound like?"

5. **Teacher debriefs the whole group.**

   "Do you see how language choices and patterns can help us to change the voice?"

*(continued)*

6. **Teacher prepares students for the physical, cognitive, and social demands of doing this independently.**

"Voice isn't something that develops overnight. When you read, try to notice what makes a piece of writing sound as it does. Then see what happens in your own writing when you experiment in that way. We will continue to talk about this and begin to note it in on another's writing."

## MINI-LESSON ON WORD CHOICE

1. **Teacher introduces the subject under discussion.**

"Today we are going to talk about choosing words when we write. Sometimes, as part of the process of revision, we go back and look carefully at our words to see whether they can be more precise or lively."

2. **Teacher talks about how students get started.**

"Let's say I am writing about a time when I was really happy with an outcome of my work. I am writing along and realizing that I keep using the words 'happy' and 'pleased,' and that these words aren't really expressing what I want them to express."

3. **Teacher models the process for students on chart paper, an overhead, document camera, or the chalkboard.**

"I decide that I am going to make a list of all the words I can come up with that mean 'happy' and that I am going to put them on a continuum from mildest to most exuberant. I may use a thesaurus to help me. Here I go:
'satisfied/pleased/relieved/tickled/joyful/thrilled/ecstatic/exuberant/overwhelmed/bursting.'
Now that I have those words at the ready, I feel more able to use them flexibly and appropriately as I continue to write."

*(continued)*

**4. Teacher leads students in practicing the process.**

"Now I would like you to take another word, say, 'angry' or 'bored,' and do the same thing. Go ahead and work with a partner to come up with a continuum from mildly (bored or angry) to extremely (bored or angry). Try to come up with at least 10 words on your continuum."

**5. Teacher debriefs the whole group.**

"I know it seems strange to stop writing to do something like this, but this very quick exercise can really help with word variation."

**6. Teacher prepares students for the physical, cognitive, and social demands of doing this independently.**

"When you are writing in the next few days, give this a try."

## MINI-LESSON ON ORGANIZATION

**1. Teacher introduces the subject under discussion.**

"Today we are going to talk about how to organize writing. Let's take a look at these two texts, one fiction and one nonfiction. What do you notice about how they are structured?" [*Students respond.*]

**2. Teacher talks about how students get started.**

"I am going to take a piece of writing from my writing notebook that I have long since forgotten to see if I can resurrect it into something by changing the organization."

**3. Teacher models the process for students on chart paper, an overhead, document camera, or the chalkboard.**

"Here is this piece I wrote on my feelings the day I was driving to work and heard on the radio that one of the twin towers had been hit by an airplane. I never much liked the way I wrote it the first time. I wonder, now, if I reorganize it by writing it from the point of time I am in now, as a flashback, what would

*(continued)*

happen, how it would change. I could also see if I can compare the way I felt that day with the way I felt the day I heard about Hurricane Katrina. I wonder what would happen if I changed it more by making it into somewhat of a comparison."

4. **Teacher leads students in practicing the process.**

   "Now I would like you to pull a piece of writing from your journal or notebook and see whether you can think about how it could be reorganized at least two different ways."

5. **Teacher debriefs the whole group.**

   "How did that go for everyone? Was it difficult to imagine representing something in a different format?"

6. **Teacher prepares students for the physical, cognitive, and social demands of doing this independently.**

   "I tend to start my papers the same way every time, so as I read, it is important for me to look carefully at other forms of organization that I might use. For the next few weeks, please do the same. When you see a pattern of organization that you recognize as you read—in other classes, in here, or at home—note it in your mind or write it down, and see if you can try that with your own writing."

write something well initially, it is always important to remind them that this was a limited learning experience because they simply produced without going through a process that might help them see their writing differently. Other teachers allow students to decide which version of their paper they wish to present as their best effort. Sometimes this may be the first draft, even when they have created subsequent drafts in response to feedback. For example Lacey might write a first draft about going to summer camp. When she goes to a peer group, her peers get very interested in one passage and ask her to expand it. When she does, it changes the paper significantly, moving the focus away from where Lacey originally intended. She takes that second draft to the teacher, who adds input on that draft, believing it is still improving. Lacey dutifully takes the advice of others, but after creating her third draft still believes her first draft is the strongest. When she submits her work for portfolio review (discussed in Chapter 10), she may decide to edit and present her first draft (as it was, or with changes focused in other places) as her best. Her teacher accepts this because she has shown evidence of revision, even though she decided she was not happy about the drafts she changed. This shows sophistication and an ability to engage fully in the writing process. Lacey does have drafts, and she made a writerly decision about her favorite and will see if the teacher agrees. Lacey's teacher will certainly see learning in this process.

If this happens to Lacey repeatedly it may suggest a weakness in group responses. It also may suggest that Lacey has a stubborn streak. Her teacher can respond to either of these. If the teacher sees it as a weakness in the feedback, she might spend some more time "tuning up" classmates by doing more modeling and discussion of giving feedback. If the teacher believes Lacey is making poor decisions about what is her best work, she will discuss this with her individually.

CHAPTER SIX

# Writing Is Revising

## The Role of Revision in the Writing Workshop

The cornerstone of the writing workshop is the teaching of revision. When your students understand the principles and practices behind revision, their writing will improve. Studies show that "students who reported teachers `always' asked them to write multiple drafts . . . achieved comparatively higher scores than those whose teachers `seldom' or `never' placed those demands on children" (Greenwald, Persky, Campbell, & Mazzeo, 1999, p. 92).

You are likely worried about the prospect of getting students to write multiple drafts. This is a reasonable concern and a reality in teaching adolescent writers who may not have had this asked of them in the past. Teachers will have to be very careful about their own attitudes toward revision before sharing lessons on it with children. Many teachers also resent the task demands of multiple drafting. Even those of us who write for a living wish, on many days, that what we wrote the first time would be enough to get by so that we might get on to the next task. And sometimes, amazingly, writing comes out almost that well the first time. Usually this is not the case, though, and the texts we are most proud of come with a good deal of labor. Nonetheless, commiserating with student frustration can be a great teaching tool. Collapsing requirements and shortchanging the intellectual rigor of going through multiple drafts, while tempting, is not educative. Teachers who are themselves practicing writers—that is, those who write for a variety of professional and/or personal reasons—are invaluable to student writers. These teachers are themselves engaged as writers and thus bring an understanding of the challenges to writing with them as they help student writers. Chapters of the National Writing Project exist nationwide and are a great opportunity for teachers who wish to revisit their own writing process as well as communicate with other teachers about the teaching of writing. In professional development experiences such as this one, experienced and novice teacher-writers will gain "the invaluable support of colleagues, the opportunity to learn from each other and from research, the time to write, and the anticipation of how positively students would respond to new classroom approaches to writing" (National Writing Project, 2007). For more information on these three-week summer programs for teachers, please go to *www. writingproject.org.*

No matter what you or your students think about revision, understanding it as an integral part of the writing process is necessary. In a workshop on writing about mathematics, a secondary math teacher was able to put revision in the context of her subject area expertise. She told a group of writing teachers who were complaining that students were resistant to creating multiple drafts that students also get tired of extended math problems. When she asks them to "first write out the problem," they groan. When she directs them to go step by step through their calculations, they attempt to use shortcuts. When she asks them to reflect on how they got their answers they pout. She understands this, validates the challenges and the time involved in doing so, yet she continues to require it because it is "the way that students learn about math": "They may get that one problem, fine. But what do I care about that one problem? I am teaching them mathematical process. This teacher went on to explain that she had greatly reduced the number of problems she gives students for practice—in class or as homework—in order to give them more time to work through this process. The teachers in this workshop learned a great deal about teaching writing by listening carefully to their colleague describe this contemporary approach to teaching math. Students might not want to rewrite—who blames them? They may not want to get feedback that will require them to think hard about their message and their manner of communicating that message; this is reasonable, too. Yet, this is the way one improves. When students write first drafts, merely edit these drafts, and turn them in for your evaluation, they are presenting you the equivalent of a pretest. You might use pretests across the content areas to see where students are in their knowledge. That is the kind of information offered in a first draft, and it can be useful to help plan future instruction. You might notice that a student or group of students is writing with a very flat tone; you might notice something about the length of their sentences, or their awareness of the audience. All this is good information for you to have. Once you have seen what your students can do unprompted, without instruction, you can begin teaching them to take those first drafts and use feedback to improve them. Students learn about writing not by spitting out a first draft, and then another and another, but by taking some of those first drafts through the writing process.

## Encouraging Revision in the Writer's Workshop

Your students will have a great deal of difficulty if you instruct them to "revise" or "create a second draft" without appropriate input to encourage this. Writers put down their thoughts the best way they know how; thus it isn't always easy to see what else could be done. You might think of the time between drafts as time to get some kind of input that will help a writer to know where to go with the next draft. This input can come from a variety of sources. Sometimes it is based on information gathered after they have reconsidered their own writing or have had assistance in doing so. Other times this input is more indirect and comes from being introduced to new ideas or writing techniques that trigger a reconsideration of a piece of writing. Students can learn about writing and can often dramatically improve their writing by drafting and then reconsidering that draft in light of time, after getting feedback, following new opportunities to research or learn about a topic, while reading the work of peers, and/or through your direct instruction. Not all writers will benefit from all of these strategies, but you will want to encourage your students to seek many different kinds of input as they learn what works and what doesn't work for them. Practice in using each of these elements will give student writers exposure to different ways in which they might approach revision and creating new drafts.

### *Time*

Peter Elbow (1973) talks about letting a draft "weather," that is, to take some time away from writing before returning with fresh eyes. Students can be encouraged to work on another piece of writing for a day or so (or at least to wait until the next class period to work on it) while their draft weathers. It is always exciting for student writers to return to a piece and delight in it, or to see where more writing can be done. Many teachers provide checklists for students to use while they are trying to resee their own work. Figure 6.1 is a "weathering checklist." Students should be encouraged to use this after some time has elapsed and they are ready to return to their writing with fresh eyes.

### Direct Instruction

A chapter in Lucy Calkins's (1994) book *The Art of Teaching Writing* is titled "Don't Be Afraid to Teach." In this chapter she disputes the notion that teachers don't explicitly teach students about writing in the writing workshop. You have a vital role in the writing workshop—not just setting up the structures and teaching students to move through those structures, but also in your knowledge of writing traits and strategies and your experiences with a wider variety of texts than most stu-

---

This is a self-directed worksheet. After completing each step, place a check next to it.

☐ Read your paper as if you were someone else. Pick a person (a peer, a teacher, a family member) and try to read as he or she would. What would he or she notice?

☐ Highlight or underline your favorite line, passage, or chunk of the paper. What do you like about it?

☐ Highlight or underline your least favorite line, passage, or chunk of the paper. Why aren't you sure about it? Can it be moved, changed, or deleted?

☐ Think about one or two questions you have for a group you have imagined listened to your paper in order to provide feedback. What might you ask them?

Use the information you learn in this exercise to prompt revision.

---

**FIGURE 6.1.** Weathering checklist.

dents have had. Direct instruction, often in the form of mini-lessons or informal conversations with individuals or small groups of students, helps students build their tool kit of writing methods and ultimately expands their ability to communicate in writing. The term "direct instruction" sometimes harkens back to the kind of whole-group, elongated, didactic teaching that is no longer considered a best practice in the teaching of writing. Just because something is direct, however, does not mean it is whole-group, lengthy, or didactic. Direct means offering students new information in an unambiguous manner. It can be formal and whole-group, as in mini-lessons, or informal and ad hoc. Students might learn a strategy or technique from you during one of these experiences and experiment with bringing that to their own writing. This can influence them to revise and is a wonderful way to learn to write.

## Reading

Bartholomae and Petrosky (1986) advises us to read like writers and write like readers. When students are told to look at texts as material that was created by a real person (not necessarily an intuitive stance), they can draw on those texts to find ideas or techniques for their own writing. Many a student has written in far more detail after reading a Dickens novel or has learned how to add suspense from Edgar Allan Poe. Noticing the writer's craft, however, should not be limited to literary masters whose writing can seem inaccessible to a student writer. Newspaper and magazine writers, bloggers, and contemporary authors (as well their own peers; more on this special kind of reading below) can introduce students to new techniques and topics.

## Research

In many genres, outside sources are necessary. Beyond citations, though, students also sometimes change the way they feel, think, or believe when they come upon the ideas of others. This can be in terms of formal library or electronic research or it can come in the form of an informal poll of classmates or of a casual conversation. All these forms of information gathering—really, research—can trigger revision. Student writers who are open to writing to find out what they think can be especially helped by gathering information from multiple formal and/ or informal sources.

### Reading the Work of Peers

One of the best reasons to create a workshop is to have the support of peers working through their own writing. In the writing workshop, students are exposed to each other's work in multiple ways—they may hear about their ideas as they are forming in prewriting discussions; they hear or read them as they are arranged in peer groups or in pairs in buddy response; and they hear or read final, finished drafts when students share their final products. All of these exposures call for an intimate look at another developing writer as he or she goes through the writing process. Many of the techniques and practices of that writer can be noted and incorporated into one's own writing. It is often easier for student writers to learn from one another than from published authors because the work seems closer to them. When one is in the actual company of a writer—as peers are during the writing workshop—they see writing as being attached to a person. This can be harder to imagine when looking at a finished product, a book, a magazine article, or a piece in a newspaper.

### Feedback

The most direct way that student writers get feedback on their own writing is by participating in collaborative classroom activities. These activities take a large chunk of time during the writing workshop, largely because they are so generative. Teachers can set up opportunities for peer feedback in the form of peer writing groups or buddy sharing, and they can respond to student writing on their own in guided writing groups, in writing conferences, and in written response to student writing. Full discussions of these activities come in Chapters 7 and 8.

## Practicing Incremental Revision

Now that you have given your students ample opportunity to get feedback, you will want to help them to know what to do with it. It is fine to teach students to get feedback so that they write down a list of things that they could do with their paper; it's quite another for students to actually do them. Students don't always know how to change their work, even with the best input available. You might have had the frustrating experience of talking to a student about his or her paper or writing extensive commentary only to see a new draft come back to you with little or no substantial change. Sometimes this is a result of noncompliance, a decision made by the student not to rewrite. Other times it is because the student did not understand what to do. The first part of engaging in revision is seeking feedback in some of the ways suggested above. The second part is using that feedback to improve a paper.

One way to help with the frustration that some students feel as they attempt to revise is to help them to isolate the locations and strategies for revision and to offer guided practice in revising. There are predictable parts of a paper that are easier to revise, and there are some techniques that are easier to master than others. It makes sense to start with those, giving students opportunities to succeed with those locations and strategies before moving on to more difficult challenges. A model for incremental revision would reflect the following sequence:

1. Adding on to the end.
2. Adding on to the beginning.
3. Adding to the middle.
4. Taking out big chunks.
5. Taking out smaller chunks.
6. Moving around.

Of all the ways to revise, adding to a text is the easiest for students. Of all the places to add, the end of the paper (for obvious logistical reasons) is the easiest. In order to encourage success, you can give students focused opportunities to get feedback on short, quick pieces of writing and then to simply add on to the end. Adding on to the end is a specific activity that helps students to see their writing grow. Of course, you would not want that to be the sole location for revision in a student repertoire, but it is a first step, especially for students who haven't been asked to do real revision in the past.

Much of the revision by inexperienced writers is done by adding more information to what they already have on the page. After some productive experiences adding on to the end of their work to create writing that is livelier and clearer, you can show students how they can use feedback to add to other parts of their text. This can be both a cognitive and a practical struggle. First we want students to see revision as more than just plopping more writing into a hole that someone else has pointed out. When deep revision happens, it can influence other parts of the writing, at times changing focus, and at times warranting attention to pieces that were not the original focus. This kind of complex revision is the ultimate goal, and helping students step through with little risk is important.

After some practice in adding to a text, you will want to go through a similar process allowing students to practice adding and then taking away material. Although it seems as if deleting would be easier for students than adding, it can be much more psychologically challenging. You might have had the experience of writing something and hesitating to delete it, even though it isn't exactly as you would want it, because, well, it is there. For students who may not find writing smooth or natural, any text is a success. Deleting something that you worked on can be frustrating and demotivating. There is something very satisfying in having words on a page—any writer will tell you that. When students labor to write and it is finally on paper, the last thing they wish to do is delete or erase. Knowing and understanding this challenge helps you to guide students in practicing taking out pieces of writing. It is not true that writing that really doesn't belong in one piece is for naught. It is probably not helpful to tell students that every bit of writing they do, whether it is saved or not, helps them become a better writer—but it is true. Students will be more inclined to understand that they can take that bit of writing and start something new that day, the next day, or far into the future. Nonetheless, it is difficult to get students to delete parts of their writing that they have already composed and this is why so much student revision is additive. Hard or not, though, students will need to be guided in practicing writing a text with a bit of length and lopping off parts. Just as in adding, students will likely find the ends of the text—the start and finish—the easiest places to cut. Once students are comfortable adding to their work and subtracting from it, they may be ready to experiment with moving text around. Because this is much more difficult, it is the revision strategy that is best given most support and introduced last.

Thinking about revision incrementally does not mean that students can't or shouldn't delete when they are learning to add or move text around before they have mastered the other two processes. The ultimate goal is for students to be able to do any of these operations as the text needs. Looking incrementally at revision is a way to give explicit instruction and scaffolded practice in particular techniques and locations so that students might become increasingly comfortable revising in multiple ways.

## Using Technology (and Other Ways) to Revise

When students have access to even very rudimentary word processing programs, they have an obvious advantage when it comes to revision. When you can simply cut and paste, adding to the middle of a document requires minimal physical effort. If students believe that changing a text means physically rewriting, they will be very reluctant to do so. We all would be. If you have even a small number of computers, you might allot them to students who are at the drafting stage (either first drafting or creating subsequent drafts based on feedback). Students who are coming up with ideas, prewriting, giving or receiving feedback, and editing also benefit from technology, but it is less vital. Laptop carts, along with any classroom computers, are of significant worth in writing workshop. It also may be worth it to look into reserving a computer lab, or part of one, to send students to during drafting. Of course, this would depend upon availability, supervision, location and the rest of the school context. It is worth some creative use of space or technology to give students this tool.

It is difficult to add to written text (written as in handwritten rather than word-processed) because of obvious space issues on a page and because of the difficulty of fluent reading of texts that have writing in unexpected places. When students are creating drafts, you'll want to do everything you can to support significant revision. The chore of having to physically rewrite one's text has stopped more than a few students from engaging in real revision. Taking away that barrier will help tremendously. Remember that as students write, the paper needn't look neat. It only needs to be readable by the author and peers or the teacher. Many students get agitated when writing in the margins, crossing out, or arrow markings mar the pristine look of their first paper. Part of learning to revise is seeing this as significant to the process. Writers make a mess as they are pushing through their work. Eventually this mess leads to clearer writing, but it doesn't always look that way mid-process.

Listed in Figure 6.2 are some ways in which high school teachers have made it easier for students to change their work. None of these are perfect—word processing is the ideal, but limited resources require

1. Have students triple space when they work on lined paper. The extra space won't interfere with their initial reading, and they will have ample room to add.

2. Ask students to physically cut their paper out and paste or tape it in pieces on a large piece of chart paper so they can add other pieces of paper in between the spaces.

3. Provide sticky notes in a variety of sizes that students can write on and place on their papers, sometimes with the aid of an arrow or asterisk. Use sentence strips (adhesive correction tape) to create space above and below other lines in similar ways.

4. Have students place insertion notes where they want to add and then create a "key" on another sheet of paper. That means a student might put a number 1 with a small caret at the first location where they have decided to write more. Corresponding to that will be a number one on an additional piece of paper that the student will have attached.

5. Pair students up and have them dictate their changes to each other. The mere fact that someone else is doing the writing cheers students enough to face the chaotic appearance on the page.

6. Give students carbon paper so they will have multiple copies of their first draft. Maintaining one in its original state is calming to some students.

**FIGURE 6.2.** Ideas to make revision easier.

creative thinking. These ideas may be helpful as they are or to spur even more ideas.

## Not Revising

You will find your own best way to determine the amount of drafts you require for a particular piece in a given writing workshop. Some of these determiners are discussed in other chapters, in particular Chapter 2 on the structures for writing workshop and Chapters 7 and 8 on peer and teacher feedback. At some point, even with as much choice as we wish to give writers, there comes a time when teachers insist that a particular piece of writing move beyond the first draft. In a chapter on revision it is worth reiterating that students may write a bunch of first drafts that never make it past that stage. For whatever reason, the student decides not to move forward with a draft for feedback. It is productive to give students these choices, because these are the choices they will face when they write in the future. For example a student assigned a paper in another course may start it several times before finding a version that he or she wishes to pursue. Similarly, adults who write for a living may spend a chunk of time on something that at some point they determine isn't worth continuing to work on. However in the slightly manufactured world of school writing courses, at some point students need to learn how to commit enough to a piece of writing to be willing to accept multiple forms of feedback and revisions, and ultimately decide that something is finished. You might deem it best to offer students a time frame, for instance 3 weeks, in which they are required to take a piece of writing through multiple drafts that culminate in an assessment or other form of publication. If this is done, students are free to reject much of their early writing before they find something they are eager or willing to share. At some point you will want to encourage reluctant students to pick the draft they are most interested in and pursue feedback on it. Students will be taught that first drafts are always tentative, and that sometimes feedback helps to shape them in such a way that they turn out to be more than the writer thought they might be. Other times students will take two pieces of early writing to a group or peer and ask their view on which is more promising or riper for revision. In any case, students learn to write by receiving feedback that prompts revision, and teachers must insist that this gets enough attention during the writing workshop. The short answer is that revision is not an option. Every student will have the experience of producing multiple drafts.

On occasion, students will revise because of feedback and find that they liked their first draft more. This is a generative insight and one that you might encourage. As long as students write multiple drafts, it is their option to select the draft they wish to submit for final assessment, even if it is the initial one. More often than not, students will find that their writing does progress through the drafts. Even if the final draft isn't as strong as the first, the learning that occurred during the process remains.

## Showing Evidence of Revision

Students unused to doing real revision may misunderstand the character of it. They may believe that changing a word or two or editing their work is what revision is about. When students are asked to create second or third drafts, it is useful to require a minimum amount of revision, at least early in the year, so that they begin to understand that true revision means significant change in a piece of writing. In Chapter 10, when assessment is discussed, you will see that change is one measure that teachers use to assess student progress in the writing workshop. If students don't make changes, not matter how skilled they are when they begin, they haven't learned as much as they can. One useful tip is to decide on a minimum percentage of revision necessary to call something a second draft. For instance, one team of high school teachers in an urban school decided that students should make at least 25% change every time they moved to a new draft. A student who says that he or she is finished with a second draft, yet doesn't have a least a quarter of the paper changed either by adding text, subtracting text, moving text, or some combination, has not produced a real second draft as required. Teachers should decide what they consider to be minimum amount of change and hold students to that standard, at least early in the year as they learn to make real change.

To easily see these changes, this same group of teachers came up with a highlighting system. They asked students to highlight, in yellow, on draft 2, everything that they added to it. They asked them to highlight, in pink, on draft 1 everything that was in draft 1, but that they edited out to create draft 2. Any writing that was moved was indicated in green highlights on draft 2. It only took these teachers a moment to determine whether enough change had been made to warrant calling something a second draft. Certainly the same thing could be accomplished with underlining and circling if multicolored highlighters are unavailable. *How's It Done?: Highlighting Drafts* shows an example of this approach. The new writing added to draft 2 is highlighted in gray; everything that was edited out for the second draft has been underlined in draft 1; and any writing that was moved has been circled. Directions given to students to explain the highlighting process are also included.

# How's It Done?: Highlighting Drafts

## DRAFT 1

There was a time when I thought that all superheroes were real. I am not sure there is a 6-year-old boy who doesn't think so. But I took my obsession a little further then most. It was my 6th birthday and I decided I was going to fly like my heroes that I watched and read about. I went to the top of the hill behind my house, put a cape around my shoulders, and jumped as high as I could go. It doesn't sound surprising that I fell flat on my face. My friends were laughing as if they didn't believe that I could do it. This made me even more eager to prove them wrong. This time, I ran and jumped into a big pit. I knew that if I could fly it would be this way. It isn't a shock that I broke my arm in two places and was lucky it wasn't worse. This was an example of reality hitting hard in the face.

## DRAFT 2

It was my 6th birthday and I decided I was going to fly like my heroes that I watched and read about. I went to the top of the hill behind my house, put a cape around my shoulders, and jumped as high as I could go. It doesn't sound surprising that I fell flat on my face. My friends were laughing as if they didn't believe that I could do it. This made me even more eager to prove them wrong. This time, I ran and jumped into a big pit. I knew that if I could fly it would be this way. There was a time when I thought that all superheroes were real. It isn't a shock that I broke my arm in two places and was lucky it wasn't worse. This was an example of reality hitting hard in the face.

There have been many times now that I tried to prove everyone wrong and I have ended up hurt. I think that might be the way that I am. Whenever I am presented with a challenge I cannot help but make a fool of myself trying to see that, "yes" I can do it.

*(continued)*

## DIRECTIONS FOR HIGHLIGHTING DRAFTS

You will turn in both your first and second drafts. Before submitting, please do the following:

- On draft 1, highlight in pink (or underline) all writing that does not appear in draft 2 (because you decided to take it out).
- On draft 2, highlight in yellow all writing that you added, so that it didn't appear in draft 1 (because you decided to add it).
- On draft 2, highlight in green (or circle) all writing you moved to a new location (because you found it fit better somewhere else).
- If you find that you have less than 25% color between first and second drafts, you should go back and revise further before submission.

# CHAPTER SEVEN

# Peer Feedback

## Peer Feedback in the Writing Workshop

Arranging opportunities for students to respond to one another's work is one of your most important roles in the writing workshop. Joseph Harris (1990) describes the writing workshop as a collaborative community of writers. Characteristic of this collaboration is an emphasis on peer support for increased achievement in writing. Having an audience of peers to write for helps bridge the significant gap between the abstract idea of audience and the reality of a real person responding to your writing. Teacher feedback is invaluable to be sure (see Chapter 8 for a discussion of teacher feedback on student writing), but the power of multiple voices that have no real authority over the author offers another important experience. When teachers respond, students tend to take those responses as sacred. No matter how much time and effort a teacher spends placing him- or herself as a member of a writing community with an opinion no greater than any other opinion, students have had too many years of seeing the teacher as authority to let that go entirely. The truth is, the teacher probably does have significant experience in helping student writers and may be quite adept at giving feedback that is intrinsically valuable. When students respond to one another, they place a cognitive challenge in front of the writer. This challenge is significant and generative. Beach and Friedrich (2006) discuss the value of peer feedback in the writing classroom, but they note that students need to be trained in both "strategies for providing specific, descriptive feedback and on group processing skills for working cooperatively with peers" (p. 228). They cite research by Berg (1999) and Straub (1997) suggesting that students who receive feedback from peers who have been instructed in doing so progress in their writing more than those who receive feedback from peers left to figure out how to do it on their own. This is not surprising; what is surprising is how little classroom attention is usually devoted to this kind of instruction. If you place students in groups and ask them to respond to one another's work as if this is an intuitive activity, you will likely be disappointed with the results. Students may try hard but have limited ability to read critically or to understand how to communicate their responses to a writer. Students may also have little experience with functioning in an academic group that is not supervised by an adult. Instruction in preparing students to participate in these groups thus must be both social and cognitive.

## Where Peer Response Fits

Returning for a moment to the way that students work through the writing process in the classroom may be helpful in understanding the role of peer response. After planning or invention or whatever prewriting technique is used to get a student started, students create a first draft. This first draft is the text that students take to peers in order to get feedback. It is best to have students get feedback from peers before they get feedback from their teachers in order to allow students to get the first crack at response. There are two primary structures for peer feedback: buddy response and peer group response. Both can incorporate written and verbal feedback, but each has unique characteristics. Some teachers have students get both kinds of feedback on the same draft; others have students participate in one or the other, teaching them to use the feedback to create a second draft. Students are then required to take that second draft to the other kind of response context. It is probably more typical for teachers to require students to participate in one or the other, not both, for each paper they write. Examples of two different cycles of progression can be found in Figures 7.1 and 7.2. It should be noted that students in Figure 7.1 are required to produce an additional draft after getting feedback from another context. In addition, the feed-

| Paper | #1 | | | | | |
|-------|----|----|----|----|----|----|
| Activity | Prewriting | Drafting | Peer group | Revision | Buddy | Revision |
| Draft | 0 | 1 | 1 | 1→2 | 2 | 2→3 |

| Paper | #1 (cont.) | | | |
|-------|-----------|----|----|----|
| Activity | Teacher response | Revision | Editing | Publication |
| Draft | 3 | 3→4 | 4 | Final draft |

**FIGURE 7.1.** Sample progression of 4 required draft cycles.

back contexts (peer or buddy) can be easily flipped if you ask students to get buddy feedback initially, to revise based on that, and then attend a peer response group. Both configurations have students respond to peer feedback initially before getting feedback from you.

Each box need not represent a single day. At times students will be able to do more than one activity in a day, such as work with their buddy and begin revisions. Other times one of the activities described might take multiple days. This figure represents the sequence of events, not the duration. Typically, students do spend about one class period on each of the activities, but as discussed in Chapter 2, much of the workshop is independently paced and there can be great variation. The practices behind the peer structures and how to prepare students for productive participation are discussed below.

| Paper | #1 | | | | | |
|-------|----|----|----|----|----|----|
| Activity | Prewriting | Drafting | Peer group of buddy | Revision | Teacher response | Revision |
| Draft | 0 | 1 | 1 | 1→2 | 2 | 2→3 |

| Paper | #1 (cont.) | |
|-------|-----------|----|
| Activity | Editing | Publication |
| Draft | 3 | Final draft |

**FIGURE 7.2.** Sample progression of 3 required draft cycles.

## Understanding Peer Group Response

### Peer Response Group Composition

Peer response groups are collections of students who gather to offer and receive feedback on their writing. These groups are generally four or five students, and the membership is ad hoc and heterogeneous. Ideally, students of varied abilities work together in the groups, but in reality, students group when they are ready. When a student is done with a draft, he or she signs up on a list and waits for the next three or four students to finish. Once there are four students ready for group, the group is considered composed, and the students move to a designated area to work on their response task.

### Task

The point of participating in the group is to leave with feedback that will prompt revision. In order to get this feedback, students read their work aloud and then listen as their peers respond both to what they like about the paper and what they think would improve it. The group has the best chance of proceeding productively if students know exactly what they are expected to accomplish during the group meeting and how to behave in order to accomplish these goals.

In general, the groups proceed in the following fashion: Group member 1 reads his or her paper aloud as the other group members listen carefully. If possible, group members also have a copy of the paper that the writer is reading. This can be accomplished easily if the draft has been word-processed (by printing out multiple copies). If the draft has been handwritten, it may be photocopied if resources permit, or students may write on carbon paper to create multiple copies. Short of these methods of reproducing the paper, students can look over the writer's shoulder as the paper is read. It is important that students both hear the writer read their work and see the work that is being read. Some students have great difficulty absorbing just by listening, especially when the work is read softly or quickly. Thus it is important that they be able to have a view of the paper as it is being read. It is equally important that the writers read their own work. This benefits them, because they tend to hear what they wrote with new ears, and it also benefits the listeners, who gain much from hearing it read by the voice that wrote it. Following reading, the writer pauses for a moment to let the readers think and perhaps make some notes about their responses.

After a moment or two, group members begin to discuss what they particularly enjoyed about the paper and what they question, advise, or think would improve it in subsequent drafts. This conversation is done with the writer listening, but the writer does not participate. It is very tempting to become defensive about one's writing as it is being discussed, and it is crucial that the responders feel free to talk without this defensiveness. It is hard enough for some students to say something that may be hurtful to the writer without having to worry that the writer will argue with them about it. The writer's main job is to listen, and perhaps to take notes and later to reflect upon what was said. The steps of the peer response group can be summarized as follows:

1. Groups of four of five students form.
2. One student elects to go first and reads his or her work.
3. Group members listen.
4. Group members give feedback.
5. Writer takes notes on group feedback.
6. Group moves on to the next person until all have read.

Figure 7.3 gives an example of these directions as they might be distributed to students.

---

1. Each member of the group should have a piece of writing to share.
2. The writer reads his or her work aloud to the group. The group members follow along on their copies, indicating with a mark places that they want to return to, questions they have, or passages they particularly enjoy. The group remains silent until the writer has finished reading the entire text.
3. After the writer has read, the group takes a moment or two to collect their thoughts.
4. Group members comment on the paper by using I-focused language, asking questions, and making suggestions. As this process proceeds, the writer sits quietly, taking notes on the discussion. It is often best to begin responses with a comment focused positively.
5. After a set amount of time (the time allotted divided by the number of group members), the writer has a moment to respond to the suggestions and ask nondefensive questions of the group.
6. The writer thanks the group for their assistance. The next group member begins to read.

---

**FIGURE 7.3.** Guidelines for peer writing groups.

## Outcome of Peer Response

Certainly the teacher is highly skilled at responding to writing and has likely had much practice in giving feedback so that students learn. In writing workshop the teacher gets ample opportunity to respond to student writing both orally and in writing. It is important, though, that peers also have the opportunity to respond to one another. There are many reasons for this. First the teacher is but one among a large community of other writers that can be relied on for support. The role of community in writing instruction has a long history and has endured for good reason. Writers flourish when they are around others who are also writing and the ability to support one another is crucial. Second the responders learn much about being a writer and a reader from responding to one another. When one student looks at another's writing and determines how the writing might be improved, that student is using powerful critical reading skills. There is no more active a stance as a reader than reading the text as something that can always be improved. It is much easier for students to talk back to texts that have been created by their peers than to texts created by professional writers. Because this is a stance you will wish students to take eventually—that is, talking back to published authors of all kinds of texts rather than accepting them blindly—you can help them practice in this peer context. It is much easier to imagine how to respond critically to a text when the author and the text are right there and the students see one another actually crafting the work. Published materials seem so finished that it is often hard for students to remember that at one time they were created by a flawed person and that it is acceptable and desirable to question them.

In addition, students behave most like legitimate writers when interacting with the opinions of their peers. As much as you may tell your students that your feedback is just a suggestion, it is difficult for students not to automatically and uncritically accept it as something they must implement. Traditional student–teacher roles and the traditional power differential make this difficult for all but the most confident students. Thus students will accept your feedback and use it, often productively, to create new and better drafts. This is a great process and one that is discussed in detail in the next chapter. What this interaction lacks is the critical thinking skills employed when students give one another suggestions. Because of the peer relationship, students are taught to listen to one another's feedback, yet are only required to listen carefully and consider it. It is their choice whether that feedback influences subsequent drafts. Students have much less difficulty thinking of peer feedback as suggestions rather than directives, as they do with teacher feedback. In peer response groups, they also are in the position to get feedback from more than one source. One student may make a suggestion that another counters with another suggestion. The writer will have to reconcile this for him- or herself. Getting varied feedback and processing it without explicit or implicit demand that it be used helps the writer to reconsider his or her text in profound ways, taking into account issues of audience, purpose, organization, and the like— an invaluable process.

Students often wonder what happens if they get advice from their group that, with careful consideration, they determine will not be useful to them. In this case, as discussed above, the writer is under no obligation to respond to these comments in the next draft. However, in order to learn about writing, writers must make changes. If they elect to disregard the changes that their peers suggest, they will still need to make significant revisions before their next draft. They can do so by coming up with their own ideas about changes. Sometimes this happens merely because they have read it aloud to a group and gained a new perspective on the piece. Other times, the group says something that makes the writer think of another approach or addition even though the group does not explicitly recommend that change. All this is fine—great, really, because it is the way true writers operate. They may get responses that they use to gauge the effect of their writing even if they don't use the explicit suggestions of a given person. Other times students remain confused about what changes to make even after thinking carefully about the group and its opinions. Sometimes, truly, a group just isn't helpful because they have an off day, the social dynamics of the group are such that students are not productive in their responses, or because despite their best attempts they just aren't sure what to tell the writer. You can help the writers who do not get feedback by allowing them to attend another group, by having them move into a buddy response context, or by arranging another opportunity for feedback. It is important that you respond to student writing after an initial response from peers has resulted in a new draft. If you continually take over for a group that does not respond or does respond, but not to the satisfaction of the writer, it sets a precedent that student feedback is optional. It is important to build student feedback in as nonnegotiable for any paper that will go through multiple drafts to publication. Again, it is not essential that student feedback be used, only that it be sought and taken seriously. You may decide to tell students that they can disregard their group's advice, but that they will still have to find some impetus to make changes. These changes are essential in the evolution of a writer and a key component in the learning process in the writing workshop. As discussed in Chapter 6, feedback is one very important thing to do between drafts, but it is not the only way for a writer to make changes.

## Preparation for Peer Response

Adequate preparation is the key to successful peer response groups. Most students are not intuitively wired to respond to one another's writing in any but the most general fashion. Significant discussion, modeling, scaffolding, and debriefing are necessary for the groups to operate in such a way that most writers get reasonably good feedback most of the time.

As in most aspects of learning, students need both examples and nonexamples to thoroughly understand an activity. Peer response groups are more complex than some learning activities because of the significant social and cognitive demands. The first thing for students to learn is how to operate successfully in a group. The student handout in Figure 7.3 tells students what to do, but it doesn't show them what that looks like, what might go wrong, and how to handle breakdowns in the group. All of these can be learned through modeling the process. *How's It Done?: Steps of the Training Cycle* offers suggestions for ways to work through some days and weeks on preparing students to operate in the groups. You may or may not go through all of them. You may find you need to do some of them a number of times.

The important concept is that students understand groups, see them in action, and have opportunities to practice responding in very controlled ways before they are asked to respond to one another's work "for real." You should not feel discouraged by the time and effort it takes to set up peer groups, because at the same time you are also teaching them what good responses are and, by extension, what one looks for in good writing. This process is thus a process of "training" students' behavior as well as cueing their cognition.

Although this may feel like a significant investment in preparation, it is necessary. Students will need to get a clear picture of what functioning in the group looks like. Following this cycle, but before students begin to work on their own papers, you will likely need to discuss the social rules involved in this activity. In particular, students will need to learn how to stay invested in the response group. More than any

## *How's It Done?: Steps of the Training Cycle*

1. Introduce the idea of peer groups and discuss their purpose.

2. Show professional or homemade videotape of students working in a peer response group, spending time afterward leading students in a discussion of what was seen.

3. Bring in three additional adults to act as peer responders for something they wrote. The adults will be needed for only 15 minutes and can sometimes be drawn from other staff members in the building. Because the students should see a real example, it is not necessary that the adults be proficient in responding to writing. They can be instructed on their responsibility in the short time that they are in the classroom. It is particularly valuable if the adults have some trepidation about the task that they can then discuss with students, who will certainly have some nervousness related to this activity. Secondary teachers may invite the school principal, a counselor, librarian, member of the custodial staff, or any other adult who can spare a few moments. After adults are through offering feedback to each other on their writing, the teacher debriefs the class on what they saw—both the participation that should be encouraged and what the adults might have done better if they had had more practice in responding.

4. Bring in a piece of writing from a former student (who had given permission) and ask for volunteers to participate in a group as the rest of the class watches. One of the students pretends to be the writer and reads the work aloud as the other students listen and then respond. Then the teacher debriefs on the student participation in the group in a similar manner as was done with the adults on a previous day.

5. Ask students whether they feel equipped to attempt the peer group with their own papers. In these initial forays into peer response, students write a very short journal entry and then just practice reading it to one another. In their first experience in groups, they are only expected to learn how to listen respectfully and carefully.

*(continued)*

6. Place students in groups and ask them to write a short journal entry that they will then share with peers. This time, students are instructed to each say something they like about the paper. The end result is that every group member reads and gets verbal praise for his or her work.

7. Place students in groups and ask them to respond to one another's journal entries by posing a question to the author. The author merely records all the questions.

8. Slowly increase student responsibility for responding to one another and the writer's responsibility for using that feedback to create subsequent drafts.

other problem with the groups is the problem of keeping students on task and productive. Teachers vary in their approach to managing this; some ideas are listed in *How's It Done?: Tips for Group Success.*

Clearly, there are serious challenges in helping students to participate in quality peer response groups. You will find this front-loading crucial to the ultimate success of the activity. Students who work in the writing workshop continually comment on the productivity and fun of working in the groups. Especially in cases when the writing is personal and engaging, students really like hearing the stories of their peers. Writing is a form of communication that connects people, and this connection can endure beyond the writing group or the classroom.

Once teachers have trained students to function seriously in the groups and to understand what the purpose of participating is, they can begin to work on the quality of their responses. Initially, it is enough to teach students to listen to one another, saving the task of giving valuable feedback until they have mastered the behaviors necessary to function in the group.

## Prompting Useful Feedback

Once students have had experience in groups, they are ready to learn how to give and receive feedback. You might find it useful to discuss some of the more common kinds of responses and to discuss in a whole group how one responds to a text. You can provide your own work or a former student's work to all class members in order to begin a dis-

## How's It Done?: Tips for Group Success

■ *Attend to issues of time.* An 11th-grade teacher asks students to listen carefully to the paper, to think for a moment, and then to spend just about 5 minutes discussing it. The teacher believes this will be sufficient time if the group remains focused on its job of offering feedback to the writer. In order to keep the group to those 5 minutes, she puts an egg timer at each group table and has the writer take responsibility for setting it and monitoring when time elapses.

■ *Assign a group facilitator.* Sometimes a teacher will ask one student (determined any number of ways) to keep the group on task. When the group goes off task, this student gently reminds them or uses a bell or other noisemaker to call attention to the fact that they need to get back on track.

■ *Place a tape recorder on the group table.* One high school teacher was concerned that students would get off task and possibly use inappropriate or rude language during the discussion. To help control the groups, he placed a tape recorder in the middle of the group table. Students were responsible for turning on the recorder at the beginning of the group. He found this to be enough to keep them on task because they understood that what they said could be heard by the teacher at a later date. This teacher felt that the threat of his listening was enough and was pleased enough by the outcomes of the group that he rarely listened to them. When he did, he put the recording on his iPod and listened as he commuted to work on the train in the morning.

■ *Have the writer evaluate the contributions of group members.* A simple reporting form like the one in Figure 7.4 can be filled out following each group and submitted as part of a writing portfolio or daily, as you prefer. Another teacher in the same school as the one above created this form and found it to be an effective way to manage her groups.

---

Group members: _____

Writer: _____

Specific feedback I got: _____

Who participated in giving feedback? _____

I gave specific feedback to: _____

About: _____

---

**FIGURE 7.4.** Peer group tracking form.


cussion of how to respond. First you will want to be sure that the peer group is safe and comfortable for all students. When students respond to one another in callous ways, it is hard to separate the tone from the content. In addition, no student should worry that his or her work will be ridiculed or otherwise disrespected. Classroom rules for courtesy and mutual respect should be followed. You may be surprised to know that it is much more common for students to have nothing useful to say to one another beyond "I liked it," or "It was good," than to lash out at one another. Sometimes we say that high school students in groups are cursed with politeness; sometimes they merely don't know what to say. If you see that students are unable to offer constructive feedback because they fear the social implications of criticizing one another's writing, you might remind students that the group does no favors to the writer by telling him or her that the paper is just fine, because revision is a requirement. Students who get no feedback often find themselves scrambling for another group so they have something to work with when they sit down to revise. Also useful is the strategy of using I-focused language. If students are taught to say, "I really wish you would add . . . ," or "I am not sure I understand," the feedback is not criticism, but rather response. It would take a very sensitive writer to take offense to a reader articulating his or her own needs. And everyone should be reminded that the writer does not have to follow the group's directions; they need only to listen and consider their responses. Continuous attention to feedback in the groups, both in mini-lessons to the whole class and in informal conversations with groups or individuals, can do a lot to increase student comfort with the tasks.

Helping students rise to the cognitive challenge of responding effectively to peer work is harder than teaching them the social aspects. In order to respond productively, a student must recognize the traits of effective writing, think about how the writer might do something better, and then communicate this verbally. As in all aspects of writing workshop, discussion and modeling is essential. These activities should not cease once students are working in groups; rather, they should be ongoing. Setting up a mock group every once in a while takes only a few minutes of classroom time and serves as a reminder to students of what they want to accomplish in their groups.

## What Kinds of Responses Help Most?

Every paper invites a different response and has its own set of challenges, but there are a few categories of responses that are common to many texts. Experienced writing teachers from kindergarten to college find themselves responding in common ways to many different kinds of writers and many different kinds of texts. They often ask students to add; they often ask students to focus on one or another part of the paper to the exclusion of something else; and they often probe students to clarify their writing. Knowing this and then discussing it with students can help demystify the process of peer response. Students should be encouraged to respond as they see fit, not to be constrained by these categories; more often than not, though, they are grateful for these prompts, which may help them to say something useful to their peers. Teaching students to use categories to frame their responses and giving them lots of opportunities for practice cuts down on student uncertainty about what to say.

For even more support, students may use sentence starters to help them to focus their feedback. Three sets of sample sentence starters appear below in Table 7.1. These prompts are designed for narrative writing, but you can customize them based on your own students' abilities and the nature of the writing assignment. The three sets represent prompts appropriate for students at different levels of sophistication.

Over and over, experienced teachers find themselves asking students to add, take away, or clarify. Students might be instructed to prompt one another to add to their writing (either with details or by adding pieces not there in the present version), to clarify their writing for their audience, or to refocus by deleting away pieces of their writing. When considering student writing, it is a fair guess that the

**TABLE 7.1. Sentence Starters**

| Prompt | Version 1 | Version 2 | Version 3 |
|---|---|---|---|
| About adding | "Can you tell me more about .. ?" | "I wish you had written more about. . . . " | "I can't really see/hear/ feel that. You know what would really be neat to know?" |
| About clarity | "What does this mean?" | "This is confusing to me." | What are you trying to say here?" |
| About taking away | "Is this really another paper?" | "How does this part fit with the rest?" | "Why not stop here and save this for another paper?" |

improvements will come in one of these areas. Teaching students about these areas helps them to help their peers. Figure 7.5 offers more detail on adding, taking away, and clarifying.

You might want to mix and match the sentence starters in Table 7.1 or come up with some of your own to best meet the needs of your students. These prompts act as scaffolds for students who are learning to respond to their peers, but they are also useful for more experienced responders like the teacher. Whatever prompts you choose can be printed on chart paper that is in clear view where students will work in their groups. This chart could be labeled "What to say when I don't know what to say" or something similar. An example from one teacher is shown in Figure 7.6.

Teaching students to use the sentence starters to increase the likelihood of helpful response is one way to encourage effective groups. You could select one or two other practices as goals for the group. Extreme clarity about what students are expected to do will be a great comfort to them and a large step toward successful grouping for response. There are many priorities to consider. You could insist that every student say something about every other student's paper. You could require the group to provide the writer with a minimum and/or maximum number of responses. It is less important what the goals are than that some are clearly stated and practiced before students are expected to use them in their groups.

A lot of preparation is required for the groups to have the best chance of being effective. It is best to approach the expectations modestly at first because, again, this is a difficult thing, both cognitively and socially, for young people to do.

**Adding on:** Much productive feedback is started by a student noting that a peer could say more about something in his or her writing. Sometimes this "more" is more details in order to give the reader a clearer picture. Sometimes this "more" is adding a section that isn't presently there. In either case, you can help students learn to note and communicate which parts of the paper are ripe for additional writing.

**Clarity:** One of the benefits of having a real audience for your drafts (as a peer response group is) is that the audience can illuminate what ideas aren't entirely clear. Writers may have much background knowledge about their topic or story that they aren't aware the reader does not have. Thus much of the value of a response group is in their ability to tell the writer that parts need more clarity, where this is clarity of language, organization, or ideas.

**Taking away:** Inexperienced writers are often so concerned that they will not have anything to say about a given topic that they write about multiple topics in a single paper. Group members can often identify that one part of a paper really belongs to another paper, and that the writer can continue with one focused idea. Taking away is often discussed in concert with adding because once students see that one idea is enough, they are often bolstered to expand on that idea.

**FIGURE 7.5.** Adding, clarifying, and taking away.

When in a group, if you struggle to find something to say to other writers, choose from one of the following:

I would like to hear more about. . . .

Can you help me understand the part about. . . .

I am not sure . . . fits with the other portions of the paper.

**FIGURE 7.6.** Group prompt sheet.

## Moving Groups from Good to Great

Once you believe that students are ready to move these groups from good to great, there are other goals that strengthen student feedback even more. You might consider the following goals as ones that students may be expected to achieve later in the year.

First really effective groups do not follow a set of recommendations from different students so much as engage in a conversation among themselves about the text. Because of this, students may be taught to create a conversation by being certain that all proposed ideas are discussed. Connected talk of this sort must be modeled and scaffolded. Students can be encouraged to stay on a topic for a minimum of three conversation segments before moving on to something else, which will help ensure that the writer knows whether the rest of the group does or does not agree with the feedback given by one group member. Without this dialogue, much of the power of having multiple readers, and thus multiple responders, is dissipated. An example of this kind of exchange follows here, along with an example of a less successful exchange:

> STUDENT 1: I think this piece would work better for me if you added some more about the party, like why was it being given.
>
> STUDENT 2: I agree, then we would see the reason for your other actions.
>
> STUDENT 3: I didn't really see that before, but it makes sense to me.

Students who have not been alerted to the idea of connected talk are more likely to respond in the following way:

> STUDENT 1: I think this piece would work better for me if you added some more about the party, like why was it being given.
>
> STUDENT 2: I think you should add more about the girl.
>
> STUDENT 3: Maybe you could give details about the present.

Because of the quick shift in topics, it may not be clear to the writer whether students 2 and 3 are offering alternative or additional comments to the writer. Version 1 provides much more information to the author about the overriding opinion of the group members. You will want to give students multiple experiences connecting their talk in order to help them do so in the heat of the moment. It sometimes seems like students wish so badly to fulfill their responsibility to give feedback to the writer that they say something quickly and ignore the rest of the group. Much better is a real conversation where group members listen carefully to one another and engage in a dialogue about the paper.

Another characteristic of highly effective groups is that they understand the difference between discussion of the topic and discussion of the writing. Consider the following peer group exchanges from students in the same 10th-grade class:

*Group 1*

DARREN: (*Finishes reading from his paper.*) " . . . and that is why it is so important to me to go to college. I never want to end up like my uncle, with no future."

PATTI: That sounds just like my brother's friend. He did that same thing.

KYLE: I can't believe that someone that young would go to jail.

PATTI: But that is what happened to my brother's friend.

KYLE: Wow. That same thing?

PATTI: Yeah, and now he can't even get a job because he has a record.

*Group 2*

LILY: (*Finishes reading from her paper.*) " . . . I want to go on a cruise again next summer."

TERRELL: I want to go on a cruise too, you know, but since I have never been on one I think you should tell more about what it was really like. What did you do at night?

JANE: Yeah, or maybe, like, the kinds of people you met. You could tell about that.

Both groups are making an honest attempt to engage with the writer. In group 1, however, the conversation is about the way the audience relates to the topic and nothing is said about the presentation or the way the writer communicated. Students are on task—they are talking about the paper—but this talk will likely not help the writer to develop the paper.

In group 2, Terrell quickly comments on the topic of the paper but then moves right away to a discussion that can prompt revision. This writer will be helped much more by this conversation than the writer in the first group.

When students write about compelling issues, their peers can get understandably interested. It is wonderful for a writer to hear this enthusiasm for his or her argument, image, topic, or writing style. Group members should be encouraged to note these things that stir them as long as most of the group time is spent on peer response that can encourage revision. Groups sometimes spend a good amount of time talking about the topic the writer has presented and run out of time for helpful response. A balance is necessary.

## Helping Students to Respond One to One

Peer groups are important and, some feel, a cornerstone of the writing workshop. Others believe that students respond much better in pairs because the responsibility is so clearly on one individual. Buddy response can be used as an adjunct to peer response groups or in lieu of them. Although this response format does not allow for interaction among multiple readers, it can provide more time to consider papers and more time for useful discussion together. With only two students working together, it is possible for the responses to be either written or verbal. Verbal response will work much like the groups worked, but with the reader telling the writer what might make the paper more successful instead of discussing it with group members. This gives the writer the opportunity to really probe the reader, another activity that is discouraged in peer response groups because it swallows up time that is needed to turn to the next group member's paper. Students working in pairs might still be provided with modeling of the activity, with sentence starters and protocol for how to respond.

High school students are often used to responding to texts by writing about them because this is a common writing to learn activity across the content areas. This skill can be used and honed in a buddy response context. In this form of response, students are assigned or select a partner with whom they will trade papers. Once the papers are exchanged, the pair may part and go to their own desks to read the paper and respond to the questions the teacher has posed. This form of response works well for longer pieces of writing that are hard to keep track of when read orally. It also works well with students who are

What do you like best about your partner's paper? _____

Is there anything you think should be added to make it even better? Why?

Is there anything you think could be clearer? Why? _____

Are there any parts you think might not be needed? Why? _____

What general comments would you like to make? _____

**FIGURE 7.7.** Buddy response sheet.

slower processors or who don't process aurally very well. You can ask whatever question you believe will help your students give each other useful feedback. One version of a buddy response sheet appears in Figure 7.7. A sheet designed by another teacher and filled out by a student is displayed in Figure 7.8.

Another advantage to this kind of response is that you have a record of the exchange. This is helpful in two ways. First you can see how the responder is doing at offering feedback. Second you are assured that the writer received feedback and can see whether the writer is able to use it. You might ask the writer to submit this buddy response sheet when the final draft comes in for publication or final assessment. Just as in peer response groups, buddy responding is usually unsuccessful if there aren't clear expectations and significant practice. Teachers might put up a paper on the overhead and ask all students to fill out a buddy response sheet before leading the group in a discussion of what they wrote and why. Done multiple times over a series of weeks, this will help clarify for students what the expectations are for filling out these response sheets.

Name: Kendall

Buddy name: Justin

**Please give your buddy some positive feedback on the paper.**

I thought he did a good job describing the cafeteria food. I agree that it is bad.

**Please give your buddy some constructive feedback on the paper.**

I thought it was too short. If he had done more description of how starving he was, like, I was sitting in math class with my stomach growling. Thinking of all the awesome food that I would have if just it would be lunchtime. Then it would be more interesting.

Also, he could use more description throughout.

**What mini-lesson do you think your buddy should refer to when he or she is working on revising?**

Maybe the one on using more descriptive language.

**What did your buddy do that you think you can learn from?**

Maybe I could do more using people talking. He has the part where he says what the cafeteria ladies were saying and I think that was the funniest part. Maybe in my next version of my paper I should put some more people talking.

**FIGURE 7.8.** Example of a filled-in buddy response sheet.

# CHAPTER EIGHT

# Teacher Feedback

## Giving Feedback on Student Writing

One of the great pleasures of teaching writing is reading and responding to student work. It can be joyful, even while it can also be time consuming and frustrating. In order for the writing workshop to be successful, teachers must be able to respond to student work efficiently and effectively. I don't believe it does anyone any good to present a curriculum that makes unrealistic demands on the out-of-school time of the teacher. If it takes countless hours to respond to student work, then the writing workshop becomes impractical and will be abandoned. Teachers who have small classes might not need to think very hard about being effective and efficient, but the typical high school teacher does.

## The Role of Formative Assessment

In a writing workshop, the difference between assessment and evaluation must be clear to both students and teachers. This chapter discusses

formative assessment and Chapter 10 discusses summative evaluation. Both of these assessments play an important role in the writing
classroom, but neither can do everything necessary to simultaneously
help students improve their writing (as formative assessments do) and
describe student effort and growth (as summative assessments do).
Formative assessments help students rewrite their papers. A teacher
responds to student work in progress, either orally or in writing. The
student uses that response to create another, stronger version of the
same paper, to try a new technique to see what happens, or as one more
piece of feedback that he or she may accept or reject. Teacher response
is crucial to writing workshop because it is feedback given from the
view of a more experienced writer. For all the things that peers can do
for one another as audiences for writing, there are also things only the
teacher can do. Because the purpose of formative assessment is to keep
the writer moving, there is no room for simultaneous summative evaluation that would indicate to a student that something is finished. In
his book *Alternatives to Grading Student Writing*, Stephen Tchudi (1999)
argues that once grades are assigned all thinking stops. We should not
expect students to continue to revise if we have finalized their work
with an evaluative sign. Carol Beeghly Bencich (1999) bases her comment on years of teaching writing:

> Theory and many years of experience have given me no evidence that
> grading—which I still hate to do—has helped my students become bet-
> ter writers. However, I have frequent evidence that responding—which I
> love to do—has encouraged and motivated my student writers and has
> also helped them improve their writing. (p. 48)

This does not mean that there is no room for evaluation in writing
workshop. Practical-minded teachers will make room for both formative and summative feedback. In Chapter 10, I explore how evaluation
and responsibility to external criteria function in writing workshop. In
this chapter the topic is formative assessment.

There are two main types of formative response: writing conferences and written response to writing. Both have elements to recommend them and elements that make them a challenge. Figure 8.1 shows
a model for incorporating both kinds of feedback in one classroom.
Initially, though, it is important to have a clear understanding of these
response forms, what the expectations are for the student, and how to
most efficiently engage in them.

| Student name | Even-numbered papers | Odd-numbered papers |
|---|---|---|
| Axel | Conference | Written response |
| Meg | Conference | Written response |
| Laurel | Conference | Written response |
| Monique | Conference | Written response |
| Tim | Conference | Written response |
| Anthony | Conference | Written response |
| Jill | Conference | Written response |
| Nicole | Conference | Written response |
| Alexa | Conference | Written response |
| Sarah | Conference | Written response |
| Jeremy | Conference | Written response |
| Violet | Conference | Written response |
| Olivia | Written response | Conference |
| Brian | Written response | Conference |
| Madeline | Written response | Conference |
| Lorenzo | Written response | Conference |
| Shawn | Written response | Conference |
| Emily | Written response | Conference |
| Michelle | Written response | Conference |
| Rodney | Written response | Conference |
| Dwight | Written response | Conference |
| Eliza | Written response | Conference |
| Michael | Written response | Conference |

**FIGURE 8.1.** Sample schedule for response to writing.

## When Will You Respond?

Teachers respond to student writing for many of the same reasons that students respond to one another's writing—to make the audience visible, to offer suggestions, to ask questions of the writer that help them to re-see their work, and to productively revise. You are in a unique position to offer feedback because you have likely had significant experience with both writing and response. While peers may struggle to come up with productive responses, the teacher usually has much to say. Having the discipline to listen or read carefully and to talk or write less during opportunities to respond is often more difficult for teachers than coming up with suggestions for students. Scholars of writing stress the importance of a small bit of focused feedback rather than a checklist of things to do. Writers absorb very little of what we say about their writing and what we write about their writing. Less works best in response.

Most writing teachers use a combination of peer and teacher response as the prompts for student revision. When doing so, students get the benefit of a peer response (discussed in Chapter 7) and one from a more experienced source. The relationship between these two forms of response is important. It would be frustrating for a group of peer responders to know that the writer is going to get feedback from the teacher on the same text they looked at because the teacher's opinion will probably trump theirs. In addition, when the teacher responds first, peer groups have less opportunity to successfully respond because the most obvious responses are already given. A reasonable balance between peer and teacher feedback might look like this: Josh writes a draft and brings it to a peer group. Based on that feedback he creates a new draft, which he shares with his teacher. This response leads him to another draft, one that he feels is ready to move from revision to editing. In this scenario, Josh gets the benefit of two kinds of feedback, peer and more expert. His teacher can expect that he will revise on the basis of peer feedback before coming to the teacher for his or her response. This way, the group responds to draft 1 and the teacher responds to draft 2. A schedule for this kind of response appears in Figure 8.1. Josh's teacher is wise enough to require revision based on group feedback first (remember that Josh doesn't have to use the group feedback, but he does have to make changes). Significant effort goes in to arranging peer groups; they are essential and not warm-ups for the teacher response.

In this model, Josh has been required to present his teacher with a second draft. If what Josh calls a second draft is actually a first draft that has had minor or no changes, his teacher will send him back to his desk for a true revision before giving feedback. See Chapter 6 for a fuller discussion of expectations for revision. This teacher only gives feedback on second drafts, preferring to leave the slightly easier task of responding to the first draft to a group or a buddy. If Josh argues that his group or buddy feedback was not useful, he will be reminded that

| Josh's activity | Peer group | Revise | Teacher response | Revise |
|-----------------|-----------|--------|------------------|--------|
| Draft | 1 | 1→2 | 2 | 2→3 |

**FIGURE 8.2.** Feedback timeline.

he doesn't have to listen, but that he does have to make his changes. Writers learn by revising, so the requirement for change is a nonnegotiable. Josh's teacher may respond to him in a writing conference done in class, or she may do so by writing on his paper outside of class. These two kinds of responses are discussed below.

## Conferencing with Students

Fletcher and Portalupi (2001) believe that "the writing conference lies at the heart of the writing workshop." Its importance lies not only in the skilled feedback given by the teacher, generally an experienced writer and responder, but also in the "teaching dynamic that most of us wanted when we entered the profession—a unique one-on-one interaction between you and the student" (p. 48). The writing conference is essential, and yet conferencing well can be difficult.

Writing conferences are brief meetings between teachers and individual students in which they discuss the student's writing. Writing conferences can have many purposes: they can be for sharing, for evaluation, or for feedback that prompts revision. This final purpose is the one that is highlighted in this chapter. A word about the other two: Sometimes you might wish to hear student writing without responding in a formative fashion. Sometimes you just want to listen and enjoy, and a writing conference is a perfect, quiet place for that. At other times, you need to do some quick evaluations. In this case, the student–teacher conference might find the student reading as you make some notes on a form or rubric. Just like the sharing conference, this evaluation conference does not involve formative feedback, although you might give a summative evaluation in the form of a number, a letter, or a comment on student's progress. The characteristics and some typical language for each of these conferences are summarized in Table 8.1. Although these conference types serve different purposes, they are not mutually exclusive. You may find that one lapses into another as needed for an individual student.

**TABLE 8.1. Types of Writing Conferences**

| Conference type | Activity | Sample comment |
| --- | --- | --- |
| Feedback conference | Helping student by giving feedback to prompt revision | "I would really like to hear more about. . . . " |
| Evaluation conference | Assigning student a summative mark | "You have done a great job with all this and I believe that you have earned XYZ grade." |
| Sharing conference | Listening and appreciating student writing | "Thank you so much for letting me hear that story." |

The most common writing conferences are those that are designed for feedback that will prompt revision. You meet for a very short time with an individual student so that you can discuss your response to the paper. A one- or two-page paper can be read aloud by the student. A longer paper will be difficult to manage in a short time frame. In that case, you may ask for the paper prior to the conference so that you may have time for a quick read. In the case of the shorter paper, the conference begins with student reading as you listen carefully, perhaps taking a note or two. In the case of the preread paper, the conference starts when you ask the student how things have gone so far with the paper.

New writing teachers are often daunted by the prospect of having to give feedback without much time to think. It is true that part of the character of the writing conference is its brevity, and, in fact, without this brevity you will be frustrated by how few conferences you can get to. You should shoot for between 5 and 7 minutes per conference. This may sound very brief, but it is actually ample time if you are prepared to progress through the conference in an organized fashion.

## Three-Tiered Conferences

While every paper will require a different kind of response, going in with a plan for how the discussion will proceed helps you to be faster and more effective for your student. The three-tiered conference approach is one example of a structure that helps the conference to be predictable, brief, and useful. In this approach you provide three kinds of feedback. The first is an initial personal response to what was written. It is important that students understand that even the teacher will emotionally respond to writing, that even more than being a teacher, you are a person with whom they are communicating. This concept can be difficult for students who are never quite sure that teachers exist beyond their role in schools. This can also be difficult for teachers who are not used to revealing emotions or personal thoughts to students. It is so important, though, that the student be seen as a real writer writing to real readers who can and will respond from their own experiences. This need not be a long comment, but it should be a sincere one. Figure 8.3 lists sample sentence starters for each of the tiers. Just as students can benefit from prompts when they respond to one another's writing, you might keep a list of prompts handy as you work with students in writing conferences. The second layer of response in this approach is one that is characteristic of a member of a writing community. In the writing workshop, the teacher is part of the group of writers gathered together in support of one another's writing. Because of this, students

---

**Respond first as a person:**
(one response)
"This is so interesting to me because. . . . "
"I had an experience that this makes me think of. . . . "
"OK, I am dying to know. . . . "
"I love skiing too; this makes me anxious for fall to be over so I can see some snow."

**Respond next as a member of a writer's community:**
"This piece would work better for me if. . . . "
"It sounds to me like this is really two stories."
"I could use a much clearer picture of. . . . "
"There is just something I don't understand about. . . . "
"You know what I think you could write more about?"

**Respond as a writing teacher:**
(one response)
"I see that you are having trouble with this technique we discussed in the mini-lessons. Do you think you need some more instruction on this?"
"You're still struggling with the length of those sentences. Why don't you . . . ?"
"I really feel like you could have done more to change this from your first draft."

---

**FIGURE 8.3.** Three-tiered response.

are often asked to comment on the teacher's work, and the teacher is able to use these responses to work on his or her own writing. This reciprocal relationship is important and is maintained if you offer your feedback as something to consider as the writer revises, rather than a teacher-directed edict. No matter how hard you try to understate your own power in the writing workshop, many students won't fully believe you aren't demanding when you are really suggesting, but you ought to try to communicate this idea. This feedback would be akin to the kind of feedback that a writer might have gotten on the previous draft from his or her peers. However, because this is a new draft, new feedback, either in response to the revision or not, is likely. In this second tier, you should use I-centered language and might borrow the same language that is used in the peer group (see Figure 8.3 for examples). In the third tier, you respond in a teacherly manner. There is no reason not to use this special, individual time to do some direct teaching. This may relate to a mini-lesson that you presented, and the student needs to be reminded to think about; it may be related to a qualitative concern about the writing or the behaviors in writing workshop that you believe may have interfered with good writing outcomes (e.g., the student was observed spending only 5 minutes revising after leaving his group) or it may relate to a new strategy that you think this student is ready for or needs more support on than the rest of the class. In other words, the third tier of response is used to teach this individual student something related to their writing. If you discipline yourself to focus on only one aspect in each tier you will find that students are much more able to respond to your comments. You will also find that you can get through conferences quickly.

The last piece of the writing conference may be the most important. Once the teacher has responded in tiers or in any other format that works, it is the student's turn. Some teachers ask the student, "What did you hear me say I felt about the paper?" to see whether the communication had been clear. Other teachers prefer to ask, "What do you think you will do next?" so that the student can think through planning the next steps. This move from responder (the teacher) to writer (the student) helps to reinforce the idea of student as author. Some teachers act as scribes at this point, summarizing what the student says on a sticky note, so that the student has a record of what they agreed on and so that the teacher is reminded when she or he sees the final version.

The three-tier response method is only one such model. It matters less what kinds of responses you wish to give than that you have a plan to handle writing conferences predictably. In addition to cutting down on time, having a model allows you to help your students know what to expect from this interaction. Like all parts of the writing workshop, you'll want to prepare students in a mini-lesson for what will happen in a conference. Doing a model writing conference or playing a previously recorded one for students to listen to can help them to understand the different parts. "Listen," you might say to your students, "the first thing I am doing is just responding. You might not use that response for your revision. The second thing I am doing is giving you a piece of advice that the writer may or may not elect to use. The third thing I am doing is reminding the writer of something they do need to take care of." A transcript of a teacher and student working together in a writing conference is in *How's It Done?: Writing Conference*.

You will probably have a lot to say to your students in response to their papers. It is worth remembering that students absorb so little of what we say at any given time. In this, you might notice many things about the student paper that you could comment on in tiers two or three. It isn't necessary to tell a student everything that you think all at once. This should be a liberating idea. Just because you know something could improve, doesn't mean you need to reveal it. Students are learning how to get and use feedback; this process is difficult and much more likely to succeed if they are given a little at a time. Calkins (1994) reminds us that students "need to be learners-of-writing more than they need to be producers-of-good writing" (p. 241). It is less important that any one paper improves dramatically than that the writer learns how to get and employ feedback from an audience, whether that audience is you or a peer.

## Logistics of Writing Conferences

When students have completed revisions based on peer feedback, they may be ready for your feedback. You can place student names on clothespins, magnets, or other objects that can be sorted. When students are ready, they move their names to the "writing conference" list and await their turn. While students are waiting for your feedback they can begin writing a new paper, write informally in their journals, or do any other task (or holding pattern activity) that you have provided for times such as these. On occasion, students also must wait when they are ready for peer or buddy feedback, so it is wise to have a plan that will keep writers from distracting others and capitalize on extra time.

## How's It Done?: Writing Conference

TEACHER: I heard your group the other day talking very intently about your paper. I know they gave you some good feedback, and I am anxious to hear what you have written.

STUDENT: (*Reads his paper, a story about his dog sensing that he had a problem and becoming a better friend than the people around him.*)

TEACHER: That is quite a story. It is amazing that animals can respond to us like that. I've never had a dog; my sister was allergic growing up, so I missed that whole thing. Because I have never had that, I am even more fascinated! In your next draft I would really like to hear more about the thing that happened that made you so upset. I get a good sense of how the dog responded and how that brought you out of your funk, but what caused that real funk in the first place? You say so little about it. I know that may not be your current focus, but I think it is a crucial part of the paper. I also think that you could help yourself tremendously if you break those paragraphs into smaller chunks. As you have them, I have to follow you for a long time before I get a break to organize my thoughts. I would like you to experiment with some different lengths.

STUDENT: Do you mean all of them?

TEACHER: I am not sure, but at least some of them. It is okay to have some long and some short, but only having two and making them so comprehensive is making me work too hard as a reader.

STUDENT: OK.

TEACHER: Now, can you say back what you heard me tell you?

STUDENT: You said that you liked the paper, and that I should add more about what happened that bummed me out so much that my dog had to cheer me up . . . sounds kind of funny now that I say it like that . . . and you want me to change the length of some of my paragraphs.

TEACHER: (*Writes down what student says in shorthand on a yellow sticky note.*) Great, now take this and keep it stuck to this draft so we both remember what we discussed. I won't see this until portfolio review in a few weeks, but I will definitely look forward to seeing what you have done.

The other students must be able to function independently while you are busy in conference. This is one of the reasons to spend so much time discussing expectations and organizing students to work on their own. There will always be unusual circumstances when a student or students get off task and the workshop will have to be halted while discipline is restored, but the vast majority of time, students should be productively engaged in their writing, response, revision, and editing.

The number of writing conferences that a teacher can have depends on the amount of time available. In a 40-minute writing workshop period, 5 minutes are taken up by the mini-lesson at the beginning, 30 minutes are available for workshop time, and 5 minutes are needed for wrap-up. You may be able to conference with up to five students in that time. Because students finish at different times and because you can split your response time equally between conferences and written responses to student texts (discussed below), this timing does work. You can learn to manage the time constraints of teaching writing both inside and outside of the classroom by balancing response between in class and out of class.

One strategy that has proven effective for high school teachers is the 50–50 response model. In this model, half the students get a teacher conference as their form of teacher feedback and half the students submit their paper for the teacher to take home and respond to in writing. You'll reduce pressure on class time by conferencing only half of your students on any given paper, and you reduce the time you will spend responding to student writing after school. In an ideal circumstance, perhaps, you would do both kinds of responses, but in the real world of multiple sections and big class sizes this does not work. This 50–50 model is a reasonable compromise for time spent responding in and out of class. The students who were conferenced on paper 1 will get a written response to paper 2, and those who received a written response to paper 1 will be conferenced on paper 2. An example of a teacher schedule that shows a class with 24 students can be seen in Figure 8.1. Students can be responsible for the logistics of this by keeping track of which kind of teacher response is required. This is not difficult at all. You need only divide the class in half in some fashion (e.g., alphabetically or by gender) and start each group either on conferencing or on written response. The next paper, you direct them to switch.

Students who find they favor one form of response over the other will sometimes try, for example, to have a conference for two papers in a row. If you have multiple sections and large class sizes you will find this difficult. It is important for students to learn to use feedback in multiple forms, and it is important for you to give every student a fair shot at getting feedback both ways.

## Written Response to Student Writing

Because writing conferences are often unfamiliar to teachers who are new to teaching writing workshop, treating them as opportunities to respond to student writing rather than to evaluate student writing is not a matter of unlearning past behaviors. Not so with written response to student writing. Over the years you have likely developed a way of responding to student work that may have included formative and summative feedback. When using written response to student work in writing workshop, your response to drafts is best unaccompanied by summative comments or marks. When you are telling the student how the paper works for you as a reader, you are not putting on your teacher hat and evaluating it. Again, evaluation does play an important role in writing workshop classrooms, but not during response to drafts. Any inkling that drafts are thought to be finished and thus ready for evaluation undercuts the idea of writing as process. Although math teachers may look at the process by which a student solves a problem, he or she does not evaluate midthought. The student goes through a mathematical process, often in many steps, before coming to an end result. It is much the same in writing. A weak draft does not always indicate a lack of learning or engagement. Students should be given the opportunity to safely experiment within the writing process before they must present their work for a grade. Studies show (see, e.g., Patthey-Chavez, Matsumara, & Valdes, 2004) that students benefit very little from written responses if those responses are accompanied by a grade. It is thus more efficient for you to do only one or the other. When you evaluate, do not provide prompts for revision; when you prompt revision, do not provide an evaluation.

Responding in writing for the purpose of prompting revision thus has many of the same characteristics as responding to student writing in a conference. Although in theory you have more time to spend with student papers when the students are not present, it is wise to keep the time spent on any student paper to a minimum. Burnout on the teaching of writing is often caused by the paper load, so anything you can do to reduce that pressure is helpful. Remember that you will only need to respond in writing to half of the student papers for each assignment, so this automatically cuts time you may be currently spending in half. Even half of a student load, though, can be a great deal of writing to read. Just as a template for writing conferences helps teachers with efficiency and can reduce stress, templates for written responses can do the same. When looking at student writing, imagine having the same types of response for every paper, and how that might speed up the work without sacrificing too much of the valuable contribution that written response makes to student writing. A template for responding to student writing would look as follows:

- Two questions in the margins per page that are designed to prompt revision.
- End comment containing:
  1. A general, often personal, response.
  2. Notes on changes made.
  3. A suggestion based on a single trait of writing or a small piece of the text.
  4. Notes on the need for further instruction.

There are two parts of the template. The first is a reminder to keep the margin comments to a minimum. One or two at the most per page are about all student writers can manage without being instantly turned off. Teachers should not feel negligent if they note to the student only some of the things they notice. Students will have a much greater shot at using feedback if it is focused. One of the great acts of teacher self-discipline is to let a student focus on one portion of the paper even if many portions could use work. Overwhelming students with feedback on multiple parts and traits of their writing is unlikely to lead to any significant change. Focused comments are much more supportive of student development and increase the likelihood that students can successfully revise based on teacher commentary. The second part of the template is a formula for creating an end comment. Formulas such as this one will help with focus (for the student) and will reduce time (for the teacher). As in the template for conferencing, it is much more important that you use a template than what its actual components are. You will want to play around with elements to find one that works for you. You also may decide to change the template based on individual writing assignments. The time it takes to create the template will be minimal compared with the time it saves when responding to student writing.

This template was created with these particular parts by teachers who tried to walk a line between extreme direction and general response. Just like the tiered response in the conference, this end comment provides space for personal response (part 1), space for a suggestion from the teacher as a member of the writing community (part 3), and space for a more teacherly approach (part 4). In addition, the teachers who created this end comment were interested in ensuring that students knew that their previous revisions based on peer comments were noted (part 2). This was partially a management tool to encourage revision based on peer feedback and partially a real interest on the part of the teacher as to what changes were made. Looking back at earlier drafts certainly eats up time, so other teachers have elected not to include this component in their response template. There does need to be some way to ensure that students do not submit a draft that has not gone to a peer group or that has gone to a peer group but has not been changed before submission for teacher response. Return to Chapter 6 for a discussion of coding papers to indicate change. You will need to be firm about when in the writing process you will give feedback. If you don't feel you have time to dig through drafts in order to determine whether a student has attempted a quality revision, you may wish to ask students to use one highlighter to indicate those areas that have been added to a second draft (and did not appear in draft 1) and another color highlight to mark what was in draft 1 that did not make it to draft 2. A good deal of color will be a quick gauge that the student did make changes. Lack of color may indicate that you need to read early drafts more carefully.

After responding personally (part 1) and saying something about the progress of the drafts (part 2), the teacher makes a recommendation about one thing that she believes will make the paper more successful (part 3). It is usually not difficult to encourage students to follow this advice, but they should be reminded that this is not a directive, but rather a suggestion. The last component (part 4) is an opportunity for the teacher to note any instructional needs the student revealed in this draft. Sometimes this might be an issue related to editing or grammar, and sometimes it might be a reminder of a skill or strategy discussed in a prior mini-lesson. Teachers have learned, though, that noting the area that needs work is wiser than actually trying to correct it. Instead of writing a long note that tries to explain the weakness, this last comment serves as a reminder for both the student and the instructor that further work needs to be done. Two examples of end comments using this formula appear with annotations in Figure 8.4.

---

**Example 1**
(1) It must have been so disappointing to look forward to a vacation so much and end up missing the boat! (2) Taking out the part about your homework worked well. It reads more smoothly without it. (3) As I said in the text, I don't get a sense of your sadness. You seem like it was fine. If it was, why? If it wasn't, can you get me to see that? (4) Remind me we need to work on punctuating dialogue.

**Example 2**
(this paper had very minor changes between drafts)
(1) I do think this is a very interesting topic. (2) I am sorry that you weren't able to make the changes necessary to make this more detailed and more interesting to read. (3) I agree with much of what your buddy said, so I won't repeat it. I would go back and look at his advice once more. (4) While there are still many editing errors, please do deep revision before attending to them, as the paper will need to significantly change.

---

**FIGURE 8.4.** Examples of teacher end comments.

Regardless of what aspects of writing you wish to emphasize in end comments, you will be wise to plan a structure. In addition to the help this offers you, the students can also learn the structure so they understand which parts of the comment can help their revision in which way. You might plan a set of mini-lessons where you show a sample paper containing an end comment and lead the students in a deconstruction of the comment and a discussion of what the writer might do to respond to it.

CHAPTER NINE

# Correctness in the Writing Workshop

## The Role of Grammar Instruction

In 1985 the National Council of Teachers of English (NCTE) published the following position statement:

> That the National Council of Teachers of English affirm the position that the use of isolated grammar and usage exercises not supported by theory and research is a deterrent to the improvement of students' speaking and writing and that, in order to improve both of these, class time at all levels must be devoted to opportunities for meaningful listening, speaking, reading, and writing; and that NCTE urge the discontinuance of testing practices that encourage the teaching of grammar rather than English language arts instruction.

In this statement, the NCTE distinguishes between teaching grammar and teaching English language arts, a distinction that may not always be clear to practicing teachers. What, some might ask, is the difference between teaching grammar and teaching English language arts? Doesn't the latter subsume the former? This question is clarified in discussions by scholars of the teaching of writing (e.g., Calkins, 1994,

2006; Graves, 1994; Rose, 1990) who have helped to refine this distinction. They note that a preponderance of evidence suggests that teaching grammar *at a disconnect from students' own writing* is ineffective in improving student writing. They see formalized grammar instruction as decontextualized attention to conventions, and the teaching of English language arts as attention to conventions when used by students in their own writing. Andrews et al. (2006) challenge teachers "to ask whether the teaching of formal grammar is helpful in improving young people's writing . . . taking into account the fact that there has been no clear evidence in the last hundred years or more that such interventions are helpful" (p. 52).

Given the claim of Andrews et al. (2006), one that is most often supported by the studies done by Braddock, Lloyd-Jones, and Schoer (1963), one would expect there to be little formalized grammar instruction, but that is not the case. Hillocks (1986) believes

> school boards, administrators, and teachers who impose the systematic study of traditional school grammar on their students over lengthy periods of time in the name of teaching writing do them a gross disservice which should not be tolerated by anyone concerned with the effective teaching of good writing. (p. 248)

There are no simple answers to why practices that have not been proven effective persist. It is likely some combination of (1) a shortage of knowledge of research on the low efficacy of grammar instruction in traditional form, (2) a reliance on norms from the past, and (3) a real concern that giving up teaching something, no matter how benign that teaching has been, will be a disservice to students. Careful consideration of each of these possibilities helps frame how instruction of this kind can be altered and offer more promise for its influence on student writing.

## Knowledge Base

Researchers have consistently noted the lack of evidence for teaching grammar outside of a student's own writing. Secondary teachers may have had little direct access to this information because so much of it comes out of research done in primary schools and universities. The few studies done with secondary students (see, e.g., Kanellas, 1997; Howie, 1979) have lacked the exposure that larger studies of elementary students have. In a review of the research on grammar instruction in higher education, Braddock, Lloyd-Jones, and Schoer (1963) conclude "the teaching of formal grammar has a negligible, or, because it usually displaces some instruction and practice in actual composition, even a harmful effect on the improvement of writing" (pp. 37–38). Weaver (1996) echoes this: belief in her contention that there is no empirical proof that grammar knowledge translates to skill in writing. Despite this, a plethora of materials designed to teach grammar as a subject unto itself is attractive and available to teachers.

### Tradition

The educational sociologist Dan Lortie (1975) first introduced the phrase "apprenticeship of observation" to describe the experience of going through 12 years of schooling before becoming a teacher. Teachers are greatly influenced by their own student experiences, which probably included a good dose of decontextualized grammar instruction, of diagramming sentences, and of being assessed on these skills on multiple-choice or short-answer tests. The image of teaching that brought many teachers into the profession includes this kind of activity and this can be a hard image to replace.

### Concern

Teachers want students to succeed in their course and beyond. Because control over the conventions of Standard Written English will help them to succeed, they feel an obligation to students to teach them to present themselves in the best light. Teachers are correct that it is their responsibility to help students with this skill. However because the skill is not learned via grammar instruction disconnected from writing, this kind of instruction is not a productive use of classroom time. Nonetheless, moving toward an unfamiliar kind of instruction can be unsettling. Teachers have no guarantee that another model will work, and they won't be sold on it until they practice and experience it for themselves.

## Helping Students Learn Conventions

It is clear that students must learn how to present writing in a way that will cue them as members of a culture that has shared protocols for communication. Conventions of writing provide consistency and ease communicative complexity. Without them, people may feel as if they are speaking different languages. A writer who wishes to write for an audience will want to facilitate understanding, not present barriers to it; correct written English is one way to promote these shared understandings. In the writing workshop, grammar instruction is embedded in instruction in editing and proofreading skills, which we can consider both separately and together as a unit. Skill in proofreading is the ability to note *known* errors in usage of English in one's own writing (and sometimes in the writing of others) and to have strategies for correcting those errors. When we teach students to proofread their work, we are teaching them to find errors.

There are also errors in student writing that, with all the proofreading in the world, they will not catch. These are errors that students see and believe to be correct. For instance, a student might reread the sentence "They was hungry" a number of times and never note the agreement error because that is a common sentence in their oral language experience. Teaching students to identify nonstandard English that they believe to be standard is a challenge beyond that of proofreading, one that I refer to as editing. Both are important components of correctness, a value in the writing workshop that gets significant classroom attention. Both are necessary steps for students to go through in order to prepare their work in its final form. Editing is often much harder because it is less a matter of looking for mistakes than remembering something taught about the nature of the language. Students will not be able to edit their papers unless they have significant instruction to help them understand why something violates standard English conventions and what to do about it. Proofreading is error hunting, something students need to be taught to do, but something well within their capacity, while editing requires a larger cognitive investment. The first important step in helping students to correct their work accurately is to distinguish the purposes and practices of editing and proofreading from other components of the writing process, specifically revision. The differences between editing, proofreading, and revising are summarized in Table 9.1.

## Editing and Proofreading *after* Revision

Traditionally, students (and sometimes teachers) have struggled to discriminate between revision, editing, and proofreading. This often causes revision to suffer and slows a student's progress in writing,

**TABLE 9.1. Distinctions between Revising, Editing, and Proofreading**

| Component | Purpose | Instructional focus | Step in process |
|---|---|---|---|
| Revising | Changing drafts to improve attention to audience, focus, organization, word choice, interest, etc. | Instruction and practice in using feedback to make changes in drafts | Before proofreading and editing |
| Editing | Finding and correcting errors in Standard Written English that the student may read as correct | Instruction and practice in noting and fixing correct and incorrect forms of words, sentences, punctuation, etc. | After revision and before proofreading |
| Proofreading | Finding and correcting errors that the student knows to be incorrect | Instruction and practice in careful, purposeful reading to look for mistakes | Last step before "publication" or calling something finished |

because editing and proofreading, although an important component in polishing writing, do not always help to make one's writing richer. Once the distinction between revision and editing and proofreading is secured in a student writer's mind, each activity can progress more smoothly. Hughey and Slack (2001) summarize the differences between revision and editing in this way:

> Editing is proofreading for and correcting surface errors. . . . Editing requires knowledge of commonly recognized rules that govern our language and the ability to apply those rules to a written piece. Such rules define "acceptable" and "unacceptable" uses of standard English. Revision, on the other hand, deals with revisiting ideas and refers to the content and organization of the paper, the choice of words, the communicative value of the composition. There are no definitive "right" or "wrong" ways to express ideas; therefore, revision is a fluid process that attempts to improve the effective communication of ideas. (p. 132)

Although they do not distinguish between editing and proofreading as I have done, they do a nice job of distinguishing both activities from revision.

Students can understand the differences between revision and editing and proofreading if they are carefully taught. They grow to understand that attention to revision helps change writing in macro ways while editing and proofreading concerns are more micro in nature. In revision, students may refocus the message, reconsider the audience, or do large, structural rewrites as their writing gains a "revision" that often comes from sharing it with a supportive audience. Editing and proofreading do not change student ideas in these same ways, but instead make them more understandable to an audience.

You can remind your students that if they go into a job interview with a stain on their shirt it does not change their qualifications for the job. However it does make the interviewer less likely to listen carefully to their message. Similarly, students can write something that is wonderful and powerful, but inattention to editing and proofreading will bring a sloppiness to the text that, just like sloppy dress, can consciously or unconsciously influence the perception of their audience. Inattention to convention does not change a person's ability to express amazing ideas, but it often distracts like a stain on a shirt.

## Teaching Editing in the Writing Workshop

Editing is the focus of grammar instruction in the writer's workshop. Editing is an active process designed to help students look carefully at their writing in the interest of clear communication. Work by composition theorists like Hull and Rose (1989) helped show that students often have a pattern of errors, that their errors are far from capricious and rarely arbitrary, and that attention to those patterns can help students to avoid them. The focus of editing instruction should be pragmatic. There need not be attention to teaching editing of errors that students do not make. Contrary to some popular beliefs, students have full control over many grammatical conventions. For instance, native English speakers almost never confuse "a" and "an." A teacher may teach for 30 years without ever reading a native English speaker write a sentence like this: "*An* big fight broke out in the hallway." To those who have grown up hearing English at home, there is an intuitive understanding of many English conventions. Clearly, it would be time wasted to go through the rules for "a" and "an" in order to prevent that kind of error. In fact, any curricular attention to topics such as article differentiation can counter the whole point of editing, which is to locate and fix those parts of student writing that violate conventions of Standard Written English. Having students pay special attention to every "a" and "an" in their work, for example, is akin to asking a student to sound out a word that they can already read by sight. Not only is it unnecessary, but it takes up cognitive space better used for other concerns. An interesting exercise for high school teachers is to take a set of student papers and note all the areas in which they use conventional English properly. Turning the usual deficit model of grammar on its side (a deficit model focuses on what students cannot do successfully) and looking at what they can do correctly can take some of the pressure off of you. Students, even those who struggle mightily with writing, have many things going right in their papers. Although English language learners often have different concerns as they edit, they also do many things correctly. Starting from a position of strength can help you and your students to focus more carefully on correcting the errors they do make.

It is not true, however, that student attention to grammar should only focus on correcting errors. Although the corrective focus of grammar instruction is important, it is not all there is to be learned. Grammar knowledge can also be generative. Students often don't have the range of skills possible to create a variety of sentences or to work within those sentences to clarify or enliven their writing. A student may write every sentence correctly but have no ability to go beyond a simple subject–predicate construction. In this case, they could go through their paper and find no errors, but their writing would not have the grace or sophistication that makes a paper good rather than merely correct. Generative grammar helps give student writers options by teaching them about constructions that add depth to their writing arsenal.

For example teaching a group of students about punctuating compound sentences can introduce them to a sentence construction that they have no previous experience in using. A set of students who learn that adding a coordinating conjunction along with a comma can tie two independent clauses together into a single sentence are learning how to appropriately combine sentences for greater variety. Similarly, discussing comma placement after a dependent clause, can familiarize students with dependent clauses even though the focus of the discussion may be on correct placement of a punctuation mark. When you think about using editing skills as the center of their instruction in English conventions you will want to consider incorporation of both corrective and generative grammar skills. For examples of corrective and generative grammar, please see Figure 9.1.

Feng and Powers (2005) suggest that teachers become familiar with the errors most common to students in their class and plan their editing lessons based on these errors. Even though the kinds of errors students make will vary in a classroom of 20-plus students, it will be possible to find some common ground. A model known as focused cor-

| Corrective grammar examples: Students learn to recognize and correct . . . | Generative grammar examples: Students learn as additional skills for writing . . . |
| --- | --- |
| Subject–verb agreement | Punctuating compound and complex sentences |
| Sentence boundary errors | Adding introductory clauses |
| Mixed-pair errors (e.g., their/there, affect/effect, too/two/to) | Using appositives, dashes, colons, etc. |

**FIGURE 9.1.** Corrective and generative grammar.

rection areas, sometimes referred to as FCAs (Collins, 1997), attends to both individual and classwide grammar learning and also delimits the number of errors students can reasonably expect to edit *for*.

## What It Means to Edit *For*

Students are taught from the early grades to look over their writing before turning it in to the teacher for a final assessment. This is difficult for students who struggle and even for students who do not, because errors made are generally made unknowingly. Sometimes students can find errors in editing that they overlooked previously, but often those errors are not recognizable as incorrect, as in the example of "They was hungry," discussed earlier. Students need significant instruction in what an error is, how to recognize it, and what to do upon recognition. Students who struggle with their writing may have particular problems with editing because they may have multiple errors per sentence and do not know how fixing one error might influence or cause another. For instance, if the student writes "After going to the store" and has an inkling that this might lack something, adding a subject can create a new problem. Suppose he decides to change it in this way: "After going to the store I went to the movies and I saw the same candy for twice the price." It is productive that the student recognized the sentence was a fragment, but without clear strategies for attending to the error, the student creates a new problem. Editing instruction needs to attend to both recognition of error and correction of that error.

Asking students to edit is overwhelming and often ultimately unsuccessful because they often must attend to too many things at once. Using focused correction areas as the curricular focus, as opposed to generalized editing, eases this concern and allows the student many more tools for effective editing. Following is a model for editing instruction based on the premise that students learn best when they are responsible for attending to only a few things at once. This model, based on Collins (1997), emphasizes isolation, focus, and transparency to students as they edit and are assessed on their editing skills.

The innovation behind focused correction areas is that students should be explicitly taught all conventions that they are responsible for recognizing and correcting. Instead of giving directions to correct or edit their work before turning it in, teachers concentrate on teaching students to edit *for* a very few conventions that have been thoroughly discussed. Editing *for* particular conventions or structures is different from generalized editing. In editing *for*, students are attuned to things to look for and are encouraged to concentrate on those areas only. Once an element in the writing is identified as incorrect, students learn various strategies for correcting it. You can decide on a very small number of focused correction areas that you will teach in a quarter, semester, or year based upon students' greatest needs. These needs can be drawn from a set of sample writing prompts given early in the year. From the most persistent and distracting errors across a classroom of students, you can plan the small number that will be the focus of editing in the classroom.

It is tempting to try to get through many errors, but this defeats the purpose of the model. You should expect that students will learn to edit *for* this aspect of Standard Written English and will learn to correct any errors of the sort 100% of the time. Teachers should prepare to stick with one area of emphasis until all of their students have had sufficient exposure, modeling, and practice and have demonstrated mastery of editing *for* this convention. In addition to arriving at a few particulars of corrective grammar that will be the focus, you might select one or two generative components to add to the mix. Students will learn how and where to add these components and also how to recognize desirable and undesirable usage during their editing processes. In *Writing with Power* Peter Elbow (1981) talks about his own process of learning to edit *for* correct grammar. He suggests that writers concentrate on picking a few mistakes that are most troublesome or that they tend to repeat, look carefully at those mistakes, and get help in fixing them.

You might select three or four areas that come from the needs of the class and one or two grammatical constructions you would like to add to student repertoires of strategies for clarifying or enriching writing during the editing stage. For example, a ninth-grade teacher might notice that her students make errors in their use of plural possessives, confuse common homophones, write run-on sentences, and don't punctuate dialogue correctly. These might be the four editing concerns that, one by one, students are taught to edit *for*. The teacher might introduce these one at a time in a series of mini-lessons, guided practice, and independent practice. Once the teacher believes that sufficient time has passed for students to achieve mastery of one of the conventions, another one can be added in the same manner. When students arrive at the editing stage of the writing process, just before they are ready to proofread and then to publish or otherwise submit their work for final evaluation, they will be expected to show correct control over the convention under discussion. It is the students' responsibility to work as hard as they can to make their paper error free in total, but only errors in the FCAs (and proofreading errors that will be discussed following this section) are figured in as punitive when a paper is graded for correctness. FCAs make the criterion for the editing of student final drafts transparent. Students know and have been taught strategies for identifying and correcting these errors. They are expected to get them right. It is unreasonable to hold students accountable for what they may not know how to identify and correct. FCAs make the editing activity explicit by grading only on what has been attended to, discussed, and practiced. (See Chapter 10 for further discussion of assessing correctness in student writing.) In order to make the assessment of editing skills valid, teachers need to understand that students aren't only being lazy when they produce final drafts that violate conventions of Standard Written English. Often they make errors because they have not learned not to, because they don't see these as errors, or because they don't know how to correct them. Students, especially those who struggle, often are overwhelmed by the task of attending to all their errors. Because they cannot do everything, they end up learning nothing, and this persists year after year. This model takes into account the fact that students may not learn some grammar conventions in a given year, but will learn others very well. Trying to do it all at once has proven unsuccessful. That is why we still see high school students coming into our classes making elementary school errors. Likely, their teachers tried to have them do generalized editing, a practice proven ineffective by their continued lack of skill. We do better by understanding that by teaching some things we elect to not teach others. Having good control over a few conventions of Standard Written English is far better than having just a little control over everything.

Two lists of FCAs selected by a group of teachers in 9th and 10th grades, respectively, in a single building is shown in *How's It Done?: Gradewide FCAs*. It is worth noting that these teachers collaborated on

## How's It Done?: Gradewide FCAs

**Goal:** At the end of ninth grade, all students will be able to do the following:

- Recognize and correct run-on sentences in their own writing by
  a. Breaking the sentence into more than one (or)
  b. **Adding a comma and a coordinating conjunction (or)**
  c. **Using a semicolon**
- Accurately use apostrophes to indicate ownership and plural possession
- Use commas to properly punctuate a list
- Know the difference between their/they're/there and too/to/two

**Goal:** At the end of 10th grade, all students will be able to do the following:

- Recognize and correct sentence fragments in their own writing by
  a. Adding a subject or a predicate
  b. Attaching to another sentence with a coordinating conjunction and comma or semicolon
  c. **Using introductory clauses to make complete**
- Recognize and correct errors in subject–verb agreement (simple and collective subjects)
- **Use colons correctly and appropriately**
- **Use appositives correctly and appropriately**

---

*Note.* **Generative** (as opposed to corrective) grammar is indicated by **highlighting.** These are skills students are probably not using, rather than using incorrectly, and ones that the grade-level instruction will try to encourage.

common editing expectations for their students in order to come up with these lists. They agreed to teach only these aspects of editing and leave other concerns for another time. If we could decide as a profession that this would be our way in the practice of editing instruction, by the time students got to high school, they would have learned many skills very well. If they did just a few in each grade, but did them thoroughly, imagine how improved we would find high school writers in their efforts to make their writing conventionally correct.

## Differentiating Instruction in Editing

Some students will make errors that are far below grade-level expectations. Students who do so because of a lack of understanding of or instruction in these conventions should be given extra support in learning to recognize and correct these conventions. For these students, you might add one or two "personal" editing goals for which they are held accountable. Thus there may be a list of class goals, and individual students may have a list of personal ones as well. It is most important that students know what they are to look for when they begin to edit. Having a list of editing concerns next to them as they edit will act as a scaffold as they begin the sometimes daunting task of making their work conventionally correct.

You may determine that an individual or small group of students who are English language learners may need to attend more urgently to editing concerns not necessary for the rest of the class. For this individual or small group, you may have a unique set of goals. Thus these students would not be responsible for editing for the class conventions, but rather for their own list of personal goals. These editing goals need instruction and explication just as the class goals do, yet this instruction would take place individually or in small groups rather than in a whole-class setting.

There are also students who walk into class without making the errors that are evident in the writing of their peers. For these students, you can draw on some more advanced conventions, teach them, and then hold these students accountable for those. FCAs can be easily differentiated for above- and below-level students, for English language learners, or for students whose spoken dialect interferes with their ability to write in conventional written English. The concept for everyone is the same—a small number of conventions should be taught directly, practiced intentionally, and assessed explicitly. Figure 9.2 shows

| Corey's checklist (as of 1/15/08) | Shane's checklist (as of 1/15/08) |
|---|---|
| Whole-class concerns: Comma splices Pronoun agreement | Whole-class concerns: Comma splices Pronoun agreement |
| Individual concern(s) Capitalizing proper nouns Remembering to indent new paragraphs | Individual concern(s) Punctuating dialogue accurately |
| ALWAYS proofread for other errors you might note! | ALWAYS proofread for other errors you might note! |
| We will add to these as the year goes on. You will be given instruction in identifying and correcting before the concern is added to your checklist. | We will add to these as the year goes on. You will be given instruction in identifying and correcting before the concern is added to your checklist. |
| You are *always* expected to find and correct errors that are obvious such as spelling errors on no-excuse words, end punctuation, indenting, etc. | You are *always* expected to find and correct errors that are obvious such as spelling errors on no-excuse words, end punctuation, indenting, etc. |

**FIGURE 9.2.** Student editing checklist.

requirements for two different students in the same freshman writing class.

Accepting the idea of FCAs means accepting the fact that students may leave your class still making some grammar errors. Historically, teachers have made valiant attempts to help students produce error-free papers. The intention behind this has always been honorable, but it is apparent that teaching students to correct all actually keeps them from being able to correct many. A sea of errors is just too overwhelming for students to handle, so they move from grade to grade, learning little. If students learn a small number of conventions extremely well, they have a greater chance of ultimately generating error-free work (even a greater chance if this is a buildingwide effort and students learn a few per year in a coordinated effort. Understanding that there are some errors in student writing that you see but don't focus on can be hard, but it pays off.

## Development of Understanding of Conventions

Most conventions are not taught and mastered in a short time. Those that are very simple do not often show up as errors in high school–level writing. Thus a cycle of planned instruction on how to recognize and correct errors in English convention will be necessary. Teachers who go through a method such as the one suggested here do not begin to assess students on their ability to edit for the convention under study until they have scaffolded them through the various stages of grammar learning. A 1-day discussion of sentence fragments will not be enough to help students do the difficult work of recognizing and correcting fragments in their own writing. Just as math teachers give students plenty of practice in using mathematics formulas before testing them on their ability to use them independently, you will need to discuss, model, guide students in practice, reteach, remodel, and re-guide, sometimes many times, before it is reasonable to expect mastery over the convention. As discussed earlier in the chapter, there is no research available that shows that practicing the conventions outside of the students' own writing helps them translate the knowledge into an editing skill. Thus practice should be authentic and tied to students' own writing. There are many ways to accomplish this.

Table 9.2 gives a rough model for stages in grammar learning and the expectation for student understanding relative to that stage.

Certainly these stages are not discrete, and some students will skip ones or go through more than one simultaneously. The importance of thinking in stages is that it helps prompt you to plan instructional activities and to understand appropriate assessment along the way. Ideally, students will be held accountable for correct editing of the convention only once they have gone through a number of the stages of grammar learning.

In stage 1 you present the basic concept of the convention and lead a discussion with students about why the convention is important and how it assists with understanding, with communicative purpose, with grace in writing. This might be a very brief conversation, for example in the case of possessives, or a much longer one stretched over many days, as in the case of sentence boundary errors. In this stage 1 conversation, you might show students a correct way of handling the convention and an incorrect one. You can use your own work, the work of a professional, or a student writer to show the error. It is not true that published writing is error free. At times, professional writers violate conventions for good reason; nonetheless, looking at those errors in the context of real writing is helpful for student writers. When they ask why they are responsible for knowing something that a published writer does not, it is helpful to explain that these writers are violating conventions intentionally and that to do so they must know the

**TABLE 9.2. Stages in Grammar Learning**

| Stage | Likely understanding | Instructional activities | Likely manifestation in written work |
|---|---|---|---|
| 1 | Initial exposure | Discussion/modeling | No control |
| 2 | Superficial or little | Hunting for correct and incorrect examples | Little control |
| 3 | Recognition with support | Guided attention in student writing | Partial control |
| 4 | Inconsistent recognition | Guided editing in longer pieces of student writing | Inconsistent control |
| 5 | May overgeneralize | Support for correct and incorrect usage | Possibly more errors |
| 6 | Basic understanding | Independent editing | Expectation of general control |
| 7 | Deep and flexible | Continued practice | Expectation of control |

conventional usage. Once a writer has control over a convention, that writer can see how and why the convention can be violated for effect. For some conventions (like sentence fragments), this happens quite often. For others (like subject–verb agreement), there may be little reason to do so intentionally. It is best for student writers to see examples of correct and incorrect use of the convention at hand as they are initially introduced to the concepts. Once students are able to pick out correct and incorrect usages and say why they label them as such, they are on their way to stage 2.

During stage 2 students can independently locate and identify instances of correct use. At this time, teachers can set up text scavenger hunts in order for students to practice hyperawareness of the convention. A teacher helping students to accurately punctuate items in a list might ask them to look through magazines, newspapers, texts, and/or trade books in order to bring to the table examples of these lists. Putting a number up from different texts and genres can call attention to the convention in ways that invented examples cannot. The goal is for students to be able to use the convention correctly in their own writing. Looking carefully at how other authors have used the convention for their purposes is an authentic way to learn to do so.

Once students have had experience hunting for the convention in others' writing, an ideal stage 3 homework assignment might be for students to write short pieces in which they use the convention. Although these short writing assignments may not tax students' writing ability, they are perfect for practicing using, noticing, and correcting conventions of grammar so that when they turn to longer pieces of writing, they will have experience in doing so. These homework assignments may go on for days or be completed in one evening, depending on the needs of the students. As stage 3 unfolds into stage 4, students continue to practice their skills in identifying and correcting this particular convention. Stage 5 may seem like a step back. Scholars of English language learners note that sometimes as students move from one stage of language learning to the next they overgeneralize a convention. Parents of young children notice that when they are learning about pronoun usage in speech they often make changes that represent a tentative understanding of the convention, hence sentences like "Allyson is in she's room" and "I goed to the park today." The same can happen as students call close attention to a particular grammatical convention. When students are learning about a certain sentence structure, they tend to use that structure repeatedly as they experiment with its correct usage. Sometimes this causes, for a short time, writing problems that seem much worse than those that were present prior to the instruction. Any teacher who has introduced semicolons to a group of students unfamiliar with their use will recall how every student is suddenly using them in almost every sentence. While this is certainly not the ultimate goal, it is part of the learning process. At times, things get worse just before they get better. You would not want to assess the correct use of this convention at this point. After stage 5, students' control over the convention increases as they continue to attend to it in their writing and the writing of others. It is only at this stage and beyond when you might begin to introduce the assessment of editing for this convention into a rubric or other grading plan.

Once you note that all or almost all of the students are at a stage where it is appropriate to assess their ability to edit for the convention at hand, a new convention can be introduced in the same manner. All corrective conventions can be handled similarly. As students learn more of them, others are added to the criterion for assessment.

Generative grammar—that is, aspects of grammar that students need to pay close attention to so they might learn to use them to increase fluency or sophistication in their writing—is introduced in much the same manner as corrective grammar. You might explain why one uses a particular construction, how it improves clarity or adds power to writing. You will then will set up opportunities for students to use the construction. Students can look for the pattern in books or magazines that they come across at school or at home and bring these findings to the mini-lesson for discussion. Just as in corrective grammar, students may use the convention tentatively or incorrectly at first and gradually grow in confidence and comfort. You will want to decide for yourself whether you will expect students to demonstrate use of this new element or whether you will allow students to elect to use it or not. When students do use it, they are expected to do so correctly.

It is absolutely true that students will emerge from this kind of instruction with only a few errors that they can consistently correct. Ultimately you hope that students would come to the point where their editing is such that their final draft writing will be error free. However, you cannot feel it is your responsibility to teach every aspect of editing. The responsibility should be distributed across grade levels from a young age. High school teachers do not get to weigh in on what students should learn in earlier grades; as always, you work with what students bring. Of course it is frustrating to watch an adolescent consistently make elementary errors. Insisting that the student fix all of them at once, however, almost guarantees that he will learn to fix none of them. It is better to start small.

This method of editing instruction is ideal for teachers who can join with colleagues teaching English language arts at other grade levels so they can distribute attention to various conventions among different grade levels. Short of this, though, teachers can still use the strategy effectively. We know that students struggle with editing, and this model offers them, and their teachers, help.

## Handling Spelling through Proofreading

Shane Templeton (2003) notes in his review of research on spelling instruction,

> Traditionally viewed as a convention of writing, spelling has been acknowledged as an important skill while reviled as a subject, most probably because of its legacy of persistent pedagogical drudgery. Spelling has long been the stepchild of the language arts, an unwelcome through obligatory guest lingering at the fringes of the party. (p. 738)

One of the difficulties in teaching spelling is that researchers have long noted what doesn't work—according to Rawlins (2005) such methods include memorizing lists, spelling phonetically, memorizing spelling rules, and reading—but have not come up with compelling evidence for what does work. It also appears that some people are just good spellers and some people are not. Spelling ability is not linked to intelligence; there is no clear evidence of it being linked to anything. A knack for spelling words correctly can be found in highly intelligent individuals and people of average intelligence. People who read prolifically may see many more words than nonreaders, yet many good readers do not read word by word, but rather in larger chunks that don't attend to the individual spellings of words. Thus reading widely has not been shown to directly link to spelling ability. Nonetheless, students are expected to spell correctly on written work across the content areas, on standardized tests, and, certainly, as they enter the workforce.

Spelling instruction can be embedded in the writing workshop as a proofreading concern. Much of editing for grammar involves thinking through sentence structure and punctuation use. In editing students must learn to locate errors and then understand how to correct those errors. Spelling involves less cognitive strain, for once a misspelled word is located, it is often easy to replace with a correctly spelled word.

Good proofreaders find a way to identify misspellings and spell most words correctly. They may use the spell-check, ideally with an awareness of its significant limitations; they may employ the help of another student, ideally with an awareness of that student's limitations. They may use the assistance of a list of words that they often misspell, put together with the assistance of a teacher based on an analysis of frequently misspelled words; they may recall some useful rules or invoke their knowledge of phonetic word structure. All of these are spelling strategies that teachers introduce students to as a way to help them become better proofreaders. Students need a whole arsenal of strategies because of the significant complexity of English orthography.

Researchers believe that a very small number of words make up an enormous proportion of the words students use in school. Although the numbers vary some, it is generally thought that the 300 most frequently used words comprise 65% of high school students' written vocabulary (Center for the Improvement of Early Reading Achievement, 1998). The other percentage represents a huge number, perhaps more than 90,000 available words. These numbers have great implications for spelling instruction, because understanding this can help you to see what is reasonable to ask of students and what is not. No practical amount of memorization can make a dent in learning to spell 90,000 words, but perhaps it is reasonable to expect that the 300 most frequently appearing words be spelled correctly all of the time. This allows for a transparency in spelling demands akin to the transparency in the focal correction areas discussed earlier. If students know what words they are expected to spell correctly, they can focus on those. If students feel as if every word must be spelled correctly or they will be penalized, the number of novel words they tend to use will decrease considerably.

One model for the assessment of spelling might proceed as follows. Students are expected to spell the high-frequency words that they were to have learned as sight words in elementary school. These words (sometimes called Dolce words) should be shared with students. These number somewhere between 200 and 300 words, depending on which list you use. You can find lists by searching for "frequently used words" or "Dolce words" on any search engine. In addition, any words that you feel students in your class should spell correctly should be shown to them. You may have some words that, when misspelled, drive you crazy. If that is so, just tell students what those words are and let them know they are responsible for accurate spellings. Teachers may decide to teach these words via spelling tests. One practical way to handle this is to have the students write the words in forced context over a few weeks. Any misspelled words may become individual student study words. These words will need to be retested after an appropriate period has elapsed so that the students might have time to learn them. These are the no-excuses words. Anytime these words are misspelled in a final draft, proofreading points will be deducted. Students are clear which words they are responsible for; they have had time to pay attention to those that are a struggle, and they should be able, to recognize when they appear as typos or are incorrectly spelled. Students should attempt to spell all other words correctly or to use strategies to identify and correct them, but there will be nothing punitive attached to their errant spelling. Certainly you might point these out and offer a correct spelling or a reminder of a spelling rule that would help spell that word correctly, but it is important that this instruction be separate from evaluation. When students are penalized for every misspelled word, they stay away from words that they might experiment in using. A student who wishes to express that something is "humongous" might change to a tamer word like "big" if the prospect of misspelling the initial word looms. Teachers who hope that students will experiment with wonderful words will allow them to misspell words in the hopes that the concern about the spelling convention will not deter the usage.

## Using Technology in Editing

Everyone is aware of the limitations of spelling and grammar checks. Despite these limitations, they are still useful as a first pass through a piece of writing. Students need to be instructed explicitly in the ways that spell-checks function and the reason to use other backups for editing. Grammar checks vary widely in their quality and in what they consider to be an error. Students should also be taught to read what the identified error is in order to determine whether the element that the computer points out is really undesirable. For instance the grammar function in Microsoft Word regularly points out passive sentence constructions. If students write in passive voice inadvertently or too often, they may want to pay attention to this. Sometimes, of course, passive voice is desired, and the grammar check would have no way to know this. Once students understand that their thinking is much more creative and critical than a computer program can ever be, they can use the information provided actively rather than merely accepting what is offered. Computers have other functions that can also assist in editing. In particular the "find" operation is useful if for example, a student realizes he has misspelled a word that is a word, and thus invisible to a spell-check. That student can go through to find all the times he used "their" to be sure it is not being used in place of "there." Especially when some words or punctuation marks are under study in the classroom as part of the focused correction areas, students who use the "find" operation will be taken directly to the location of the usage. Perhaps a student wants to find all of the commas in order to check that they are used, when necessary, with a coordinating conjunction. Rather than page through the whole document and risk missing some, "find" takes the student to every instance of the requested word or character.

# CHAPTER TEN

# Evaluating Student Work

## Giving Students Summative Feedback

Chapters 7 and 8 focused on formative response, that is, peer and teacher feedback that leads students to improve their writing by providing them with response from a real audience. This chapter discusses the summative response that students receive when they are finished with a piece of writing. Evaluating student work is necessary and appropriate even in a context like the writing workshop that places such a premium on writer's control of their own work. Literacy scholars (see Bisei, Brenner, McVee, Pearson, & Sarroub, 1997) have pushed practitioners to consider whether their assessments in reading and writing are aligned with their practice. Concerns such as instructional validity, reliability, and diversity predominate in the literature on assessment. For the writing workshop, these concerns are clear. The evaluation of the work must be authentically grounded in real-world literacy tasks. Because the focus in the writing workshop is real writing, looking at that writing as a piece that might be read outside the classroom in the real world and evaluating it on that basis will ensure a measure of authenticity. When assessments are instructionally valid, they both promote and reflect best practices in instruction. Assessing a piece of writing on the basis, for example, only of correct spelling would not be instructionally valid because writing process instruction does not rely solely upon that single element. When assessments are valid and authentic, they reflect the tacit principles we have put forward by the kinds of assignments we have given and the kinds of feedback we have provided. Openness in assessments means that the requirements are transparent. This can be very difficult with a discipline as subjective as writing. It is not easy to explain what one means by, for instance, "writing at grade level" or "writing with voice," as these can be amorphous concepts to even very experienced teachers. Many teachers have tried to solve this conundrum of requirements with the introduction of student-friendly rubrics. Although this is certainly a reasonable thing to provide for students in order to display what measures they are judged against, this does not solve the problem of transparency. Many rubrics ask teachers to distinguish between a paper that "is successful" on a set of traits, or "is somewhat successful," or "is very successful." Teachers will differ on their opinions on this just as they will differ on grades given without the use of a rubric. Diversity in assessment relates closely to instructional validity. It is not reasonable to ask students to improve their own writing and then compare them directly to one another. Because students come into the classroom with variable abilities, and because learning to write is learning about a process, not just creating a product, it is important that assessments have some element of individuality so that teachers can customize at least some part of their evaluation to the progress of the individual student rather than only to an external standard. Finally, client-centeredness suggests that the assessments we do be meaningful, not only to students but to their parents, other teachers, administrators in our buildings, and the public at large. Elaborate coding and inbred shortcuts for assessing student writing may work in the short term, but can be difficult to use in a larger context.

## Using Portfolios for Summative Feedback

One way to manage the complexities of evaluation and summative assessment is via a portfolio approach. Portfolios of student work can be cumbersome to create, to read through, to grade, and to store. State boards of education that years ago required portfolios in lieu of or in addition to standardized tests found that sometimes the physical space it took to store them was prohibitive. Teachers and students also can feel overwhelmed when they are asked to create portfolios for multiple courses and for multiple purposes. With all those caveats, the writing portfolio remains an essential component in the writing workshop.

In writing classrooms the portfolio is essential because it is an acknowledgment of the power of the writing process. The idea of a portfolio comes from fine-arts education where students create a large body of work and then decide which pieces represent their best efforts. There is an assumption that not all pieces will necessarily turn out as a student might wish. There is also an assumption that just because a piece isn't entirely successful doesn't mean that learning didn't happen in its creation. In fact one important skill in the compilation of a portfolio is looking through past work and reflecting on why it is or is not appropriate for the portfolio. Portfolios are not merely containers where students hold their writing. A portfolio is a container that holds work that students *have selected* for public viewing and is a subset of all the writing they have done in class. If students are unable to select the work they put into their portfolio, it becomes a writing folder. Student choice is the first element in a writing portfolio.

The other distinguishing feature of a writing portfolio is student voice. A portfolio is not merely a collection of papers. It is a collection of papers that the student has selected and commented on. This commentary is often done via a portfolio cover sheet or written introduction, but it can also be done verbally as students and teachers sit together. Portfolio review, the process by which a student presents his or her portfolio to the teacher, is an important touchpoint in the writing classroom not only because it is an opportunity to describe the students' work to the present, but also because it teaches the students about their own writing. The process of looking at all the writing one has done over a period of time, deciding what to present, and pointing to the positive elements of what one has chosen can be a powerful lesson in audience, purpose, and the traits of writing. The student must make decisions about the audience to whom he is showing his work (the teacher and perhaps a parent or other student), he must decide on the purpose for the writing (to show off progress, to make a communicative point), and he must determine what traits of writing he can highlight to show growing expertise. After doing all this, the student writes an introduction to the work or plans the conversation he will have with the audience. Altogether, this is a significant lesson and an authentic literacy experience.

A portfolio review sheet used by one high school teacher can be found in Figure 10.1.

You might wonder how often to go through portfolio review. Generally, three times a year is sufficient. Some teachers decide they will do it only twice, and that largely depends on the responsibilities for the submission of grades to an outside audience (e.g., on a report card) and on the time it takes for the teacher to do the reviews. In a three-per-year review process, the teacher looks at the portfolio in November, in February, and in late May or early June. The November portfolio will be thin, because September is taken up by working through the classroom behaviors and writing practices necessary for productive workshops (as discussed in Chapter 2), and so the real writing often does not begin until October.

Even though the first portfolio review will be based on just a little bit of writing, it is important for students to get a clear view of the expectations for a portfolio review, and this experience is good for doing so. The teacher will need to adjust the requirements for portfolio contents based on the amount of writing the student has done. Because student selection is so important, there should be enough writing so that students can omit at least one of their pieces and still meet the required criterion for the review. For example a teacher might determine that each student will present two of their three finished pieces during the November portfolio review. In order to do this, there must be enough time for most students to have completed three pieces. Since

---

1. Please explain why you have chosen the enclosed pieces for your portfolio review. _____

_____

2. What do you feel your writing is most effective in doing? _____

_____

3. What part of the writing process do you believe has been most helpful to you in the creation of these pieces? _____

_____

4. What are your goals for your next portfolio review? _____

_____

**FIGURE 10.1.** Portfolio cover sheet.

each piece takes about 3 weeks given the 3-day-per-week workshop schedule, it will be a good number of weeks into the school year before the first available checkpoint for portfolio review arises. Future portfolio reviews will build on this one, so the reviews later in the year will contain much more writing and will show longitudinal growth for students who are engaged in their writing.

It should be clear that one important purpose for portfolio review is so that students can review their work and see what they have accomplished. The other important purpose is so that you can do a formal evaluation of finished work. Recall from Chapter 8, on teacher response, that it is inefficient to give both formative and summative feedback at the same time. Because you have engaged in formative feedback during writing workshop with students, you will already be familiar with the pieces the student is sharing, so reading them won't take long. The most illuminating part of this process is often what the student has to say about those pieces. You'll likely limit your written response to a very brief comment (if any) and a summative mark. Ideally, you will be able to have a short conversation with students following their review of the work, and in that conversation the student can learn about his or her overall progress. Absent this possibility, a general comment about improvement and goals for the future should do fine. Remember that you have given every paper either verbal or written feedback already. Your goal in this process is to review final drafts to see whether the students used feedback or changed their papers in significant ways. You will also attend to the quality of their editing, but again, this will require only a quick read. Once you have reviewed the portfolio, the feedback should be in the form of a number or a grade, perhaps based upon a rubric or other heuristic that you share with students.

In order for you to have a clear picture of student progress in the writing workshop, there must be a set of materials available for perusal. Depending on your particular requirements for a final draft, these materials might include all rough drafts, buddy feedback sheet, prewriting, and false starts. Whatever writing a student has done to get to the final draft should be included in a packet with the final draft on top. If this is done, you can flip through each packet and see student progress within one paper and, by looking at more than one packet, across final drafts. One very organized teacher gave her students a checklist to be sure everything she wanted to look at would be in the portfolio. This can be seen in *How's It Done?: Portfolio Contents Checklist.*

---

## How's It Done?: Portfolio Contents Checklist

Please review the following to be sure your portfolio is complete. I should find:

- Portfolio cover sheet
- At least *three* complete papers stapled together in the following order from top to bottom:
  - Best, edited draft on top
  - Previous drafts in the following order:
    Draft 3
    Draft 2 (with my writing on it or notes from our conference)
    Draft 1 (with notes from your peer group meeting)
    All prewriting
    All buddy response sheets

You may elect in which order you would like to present your papers. You need not put the most recent first. Think about how you would like to represent yourself. Of your five papers, at least three are required. Submit more if you like, but all submissions must have the above components.

Please check and double-check. Without the history of your paper, I cannot fairly evaluate your work.

---

## Assigning Grades in the Writing Workshop

If writing evaluation is going to be valid, it must be based on the values that students have learned. Because much energy goes into the process of writing, much energy must go into evaluating that process. You will want to account for both a student's individual process and his or her final products in the final evaluation. This sounds logical but deserves careful consideration in its actual implementation. Imagine two students: The first, Karen, walks into classroom writing above grade level. The second, Thomas, walks into a classroom writing at a level far below grade level. In a traditional classroom, before any instruction has begun, Karen has an advantage as her grade is already above a "C."

A teacher would be hard-pressed to give a low grade to a student with the ability to write well, whether that ability is a natural gift, the result of hard work (or good instruction) in previous courses, or some combination of these elements. Nonetheless, Karen will in all likelihood do fine, and you can predict that before any instruction begins. Imagine that Karen spends the whole year without really engaging in improving her writing, satisfied that she writes well enough to get through the class. She may not get the "A" that she was capable of, had she decided to dig in, but she probably will get an "A–" in spite of minimal effort and minimal progress.

Now turn to a student like Thomas in this same classroom. If Thomas comes in writing at a low level, yet learns and progresses a phenomenal amount, he may still not come up to grade level, despite his hard work. Traditionally, Thomas gets a lower grade than Karen even though he succeeded more fully in his learning. As we have all been told, and as many of us tell students, life isn't fair. People have varied incoming abilities for numerous reasons, and people work with what they have. However, there is a way to hold Karen accountable for improving, even on work that is good enough, and also to reward Thomas for tremendous effort, even if that effort did not get him where he needs to be.

The 50–50 model of evaluating writing ameliorates some of this disparity and builds equity for both Thomas and Karen. Students are given two equally weighted marks that are combined to create their final points or grade. Half of their grade is based on progress relative to their own incoming abilities. Student work is noted for evidence of growth from draft to draft in a single piece of writing and from first draft to first draft and last draft to last draft on multiple writing assignments. More detail on this is below. Students get a grade that represents improvement as defined by the difference between where they are at the time of the evaluation and where they were at the beginning of the course.

The other half of the grade is based on success at writing as measured by an external standard (generally grade-level standards). In this measure, students' final drafts must fit the criteria laid out by the teacher for all students regardless of incoming skill. This model works in the following way for Karen and Thomas. Karen will likely receive a low grade for her own progress because it has been minor. Even when taking into account the ceiling effect (students who start off higher have less room to grow), Karen really didn't do the job of learning more

**TABLE 10.1. Comparing Student Grades**

| Student | Progress | Product | Final |
|---------|----------|---------|-------|
| Karen   | C        | A       | B     |
| Thomas  | A        | C       | B     |

about her own writing as evidenced by little change in her writing from the beginning of the year until the time of portfolio review. On the other measure, the one that places her against an external standard, she does quite well. Half of her grade will be on the low side because of her low amount of progress. The other half will be on the higher side because her writing is competent for her grade level. The two averaged together will make up her final evaluation. Thomas will do well on the first measure because he has improved his writing, but he will still earn a low mark on the second element because his writing needs to improve in order for it to be at grade level. It would not be unusual for Thomas and Karen to get the same final grade, but clearly for different reasons. A summary of Thomas's and Karen's evaluations is shown in Table 10.1.

It is no small adjustment to think about evaluation in this way. The first measure, the measure of progress (sometimes called the measure of process), can be difficult to identify. How does a student show that he or she has learned?

## Evaluating Progress

The evidence for progress will lie in the amount of change occurring from first to final draft and the amount of progress evident between a first draft written early in the year and one written later. When students present their portfolios for review, they submit final drafts with all supporting materials (e.g., early drafts, buddy response sheets, prewriting). In doing so they show a history of the paper from beginning to end. In order to show progress in writing, there must be change. Recall that no matter how competent a student is in writing, the first draft is what a student can do before going through the steps of the writing process. Because the curriculum of the writing workshop is the process—that is, learning how to plan, draft, revise, give and receive feedback, edit, and proofread—the student must show that he or she has done so. Lucy Calkins (1994) tells us that it is much more important to teach for tomorrow than only for today when she writes "It's far better to suggest a strategy a student might add to her repertoire than a one-shot solution" (p. 228). What she means is that no individual piece of writing is so important that it can't be used to help students work through the writing process, to help them learn. Students sometimes complain that their final draft is actually weaker than their first, that all the feedback and revision muddied their original ideas. Sometimes this is an accurate characterization. In the measure of progress, however, this does not matter. It only matters that the student is learning how to go through the process and can show evidence of this.

Practically, then, there are two ways to measure progress. The first is to look at change within one writing assignment. This includes looking at how the student has represented his or her planning and then examining the changes in drafts all the way to the final, edited version. In looking at this, the real measure is quantitative change. Qualitative change is also important, but is measured elsewhere. In order to give students like Thomas credit for making progress on learning a process, any change has to be counted.

The second measure of progress is to look across writing assignments chronologically. If Thomas, for instance, is engaging in the writing process, there will be evidence that over time his first drafts improve, his middle drafts improve, and his final drafts improve. Because improvement is a measure of quality, the qualitative nature of the changes is accounted for in this measure. This half of the final evaluation, the progress half, will look both within a single writing project and across projects to give students the greatest opportunity for a thorough evaluation of their work in the writing classroom. These two methods of evaluating process along with suggestions for point values or grade equivalents are summarized in Table 10.2.

## Evaluating Product

In the end, there is always a responsibility to alert students to their academic position relative to their peers. Traditionally, this is the only element figured into a student grade. In this 50–50 model, as stated earlier, this is only half of the final evaluation. It is popular to use rubrics to evaluate student work because they are believed to make criteria

**TABLE 10.2. Two Measures of Process**

| Look at . . . | To determine . . . | And grade on . . . | For example . . . | |
|---|---|---|---|---|
| The difference between a first draft of a paper and its final draft | Whether the student has used feedback and the writing process to work on writing | The student's quantity of change | Percentage of chance:<br>Over 30<br>20–30<br>10–20<br>Under 10 | 10 points (or A)<br>8 points (or B)<br>6 points (or C)<br>4 points (or F) |
| The difference between a first draft early in the year and one later | Whether the student is able to transfer learning from writing one paper to future tasks | Your assessment of the improvement | Much improvement<br>10 points (or A)<br>Good improvement<br>8 points (or B)<br>Some improvement<br>6 points (or C)<br>Little improvement<br>4 points (or F) | |

more explicit for students. Rubrics also help to discipline teachers who may be reading many student papers at one sitting and need a tool with which to standardize their evaluation. The difficulty with rubrics is in the erroneous assumption that they take the subjectivity out of evaluation. Student evaluation will always have a level of subjectivity. Many rubrics operate holistically, and thus ask for a single number to describe all the elements of writing. If students have done well on one element of writing, for example voice, yet been less successful in another element, for example editing, this is masked in a holistic evaluation, although that student might learn about this from a teacher comment. If a student earns a 4 for voice and a 2 for editing, does that average out to a 3? Other rubrics are more analytic in asking teachers to rate student writing on the basis of individual elements, sometimes a very few and sometimes many. These can be difficult because of the gradations between the ratings. What is the difference, for example, between *well organized* and *organized*? No rubric is perfect, and none guarantee an objective response, but all can offer a level of specificity that is helpful. An example of the subdivision of evaluation product is shown in Table 10.3. The manner by which a teacher might combine these is suggested in Figure 10.2.

Rubrics can be found in many places; the most helpful are often located on state board of education websites as templates they use for

**TABLE 10.3. Two Measures of Product**

| Look at . . . | To determine . . . | And grade on . . . | For example ... | |
|---|---|---|---|---|
| The overall quality of the paper, including voice, organization, word choice, sentence fluency, audience awareness | Whether the student can effectively communicate a point that is meaningful | This success relative to standards or grade-level expectation | Above grade level 10 points (or A) At grade level 8 points (or B) Below grade level 6 points (or C) Far below grade level 4 points (or F) | |
| The correctness of the paper | Whether the student can edit for the required elements and proofread effectively | The number of errors | 0–1 errors<br>2–3 errors<br>4–5 errors<br>6+ errors | 10 points (or) A<br>8 points (or) B<br>6 points (or) C<br>4 points (or) F |

evaluating standardized test writing. ACT and SAT also provide their rubrics. Figure 10.3 is an example of a holistic measure put out by ACT. To view the SAT rubric please go to www.eprep.com/2006/12/04/sat-essay-rubric; (retrieved September 16, 2008). Figure 10.4 is an example of an analytic rubric taken from the 6+1 Trait Writing program.

Finally, in *How's It Done?: High School Grading Rubric*, you can view a homegrown rubric designed by high school teachers who were interested in a general rough cut between students. In this one the grain size is quite large, and there is less to distinguish between students. Its value is that it cuts down much of the decision making needed and it is useful in order to standardize student evaluations across graders. Some teachers wish to align their rubrics with one another across classrooms or grade levels. Rubrics such as this one can help because they are less sensitive to individual teacher preferences. Some may find this grain size too large because it doesn't

| Name | Process mark | | Product mark | | Final mark |
|---|---|---|---|---|---|
| Corrine | 1st to 1st 8 | 1st to final 8 | Meaningful 10 | Correct 6 | 32/40 B |

**FIGURE 10.2.** Sample of total points figured for Corrine.

Score = 6. Essays within this score range demonstrate effective skill in responding to the task.

Score = 5. Essays within this score range demonstrate competent skill in responding to the task.

Score = 4. Essays within this score range demonstrate adequate skill in responding to the task.

Score = 3. Essays within this score range demonstrate some developing skill in responding to the task.

Score = 2. Essays within this score range demonstrate inconsistent or weak skill in responding to the task.

Score = 1. Essays within this score range show little or no skill in responding to the task.

No Score = 0. Blank, off topic, illegible, not in English, or void.

**FIGURE 10.3.** ACT writing rubric. Retrieved September 3, 2007, from *www.act. org/aap/writing/highschool/download.html*. Reproduced with permission from ACT Communications.

**5** This paper is clear and focused. It holds the reader's attention. Relevant anecdotes and details enrich the central theme.

**5** The organizational structure of this paper enhances and showcases the central idea or theme of the paper; includes a satisfying introduction and conclusion.

**5** The writer of this paper speaks directly to the reader in a manner that is individual, compelling, engaging, and has personality.

**3** The writer is beginning to define the topic, even though development is still basic or general.

**3** The organizational structure is strong enough to move the reader through the text without too much confusion.

**3** The writer seems sincere, but not fully engaged or involved. The result is pleasant or even personable, but not compelling.

**1** The paper has no clear sense of purpose or central theme. The reader must make inferences based on sketchy or missing details.

**1** The writing lacks a clear sense of direction.

**1** The writer seems indifferent, uninvolved, or distanced from the topic and/or the audience.

**FIGURE 10.4.** 6+1 Trait Writing. Retrieved August 28, 2008, from *www.nwrel. org/assessment/pdfRubrics/6plus1traits.PDF*. With permission from the Northwest Regional Educational Laboratory.

## *How's It Done?: High School Grading Rubric*

All papers will be scored on a 5-point scale. Students either get or do not get a point for each of the following components of writing. There is no partial credit. Err on the side of the student in all cases.

### IDEA

1 point—Evidence of an idea worthy of time and effort. Ask yourself: Is there a controlling idea or thesis?

*Yes = 1 point; No = 0 points*

### ORGANIZATION

1 point—Evidence of the importance of a start, a body, and an end (but not necessarily the formal articulation of such). Ask yourself: Is there a coherent central story?

*Yes = 1 point; No = 0 points*

### AUDIENCE

1 point—Evidence that the student writes as if he or she understands that people will be reading this and thus uses appropriate explanation of details, sensory imagery, and appropriate tone and word choice. Ask yourself: Are my reading needs reasonably well acknowledged?

*Yes = 1 point; No = 0 points*

### FLUENCY

1 point—Variety of sentences and structures that help the work sound competent and confident. Ask yourself: Do the sentences move with reasonable grace?

*Yes = 1 point; No = 0 points*

*(continued)*

---

## CONVENTIONS

1 point—Grammar, mechanics, and spelling are not an issue. The reader is not distracted by them as he or she reads. There may be errors, but they do not detract very much from the message. Ask yourself: Am I distracted by errors?

*Yes = 0 points; No = 1 point*

---

distinguish in fine ways between students; others may appreciate its brevity and clarity.

Using one of the rubrics displayed here, or ones like them, will help teachers work with their students so that the assessment methodology is as transparent as possible. One way to help students to understand the portfolio review process is to give them a portfolio from a former student (with name removed) and have them rate the writing portfolio based on its process and then with a rubric based on its product. It is worth repeating that rubrics like these represent only part of the students' work in the class; the other is represented in the process grade. A system for combining all the elements of assessment in a writing workshop is shown in Table 10.4.

It is worth noting that implicit in the portfolio system is the notion that a student's collective work is more relevant than any individual paper. Individual papers get written and/or oral feedback but do not receive individual marks in most writing process classrooms. The portfolio is the product of the student work complete with students' own voice advocating for their own writing.

**TABLE 10.4. Suggested Assessment Breakdown**

| Measure | Artifact | Percent of final grade |
|---------|----------|------------------------|
| Progress | First draft to first draft over time | 25% |
|  | First draft to final draft in all papers | 25% |
| Process | Final draft content | 25% |
|  | Final draft correctness | 25% |

# A Word about Publishing

Most discussions of the writing process include publishing as the final step in the writing process. There are myriad ways to publish student work if we broaden the definition of publication to include any instance in which a student presents work as finished. This can include activities like reading aloud to a group, blogging, making a book, or submitting work to a journal. It can also include presenting a portfolio—in essence saying, this is the best I can do right now; this work, for now, is finished. Many elementary teachers spend a good deal of class time asking students to sit in the "author's chair" in order to read and share finished work. When students share in this way, they are not looking for evaluative feedback; instead, they share a piece of writing for the sake of sharing. You will want to think carefully about whether you wish to require this of all students at some point during the year, whether you prefer to ask only for volunteers, or whether you wish to forgo this practice. Some suggestions for ways to publish student work are as follows:

- Place in public space in classroom.
- Read aloud to fellow students.
- Read aloud to others (e.g., another class, seniors at a retirement center, family members).
- Publish in periodical (school or other).
- Publish in class-produced periodical.
- Place on website, MySpace page, or blog.
- Share with individuals (e.g., principal, a former teacher, a neighbor).

# Using Technology in Student Publishing

Sprinkled throughout this discussion of teaching the writing workshop in the high school have been references to the use of new technologies to assist students as they learn to write. Refer back to Chapters 4, 5, 6, and 9 for particular ideas for using technology in the invention, drafting, revision, and editing stages, respectively, of the writing workshop. See Chapter 2 for ideas about helping to negotiate shared computer resources when students outnumber computers in writing workshop.

Computer software and Web-based tools are perhaps the most obvious in their influence on how a student takes a paper to publication. Even in the simplest of ways, technology has changed the way a finished paper looks. We no longer have to rely on students' ability to print neatly to come up with a polished finished product. Nearly every public document in the adult word is word processed, and we do high school students no favors if we don't insist that their finished products be presented this same way. Even in the most underresourced schools, students have access to rudimentary word processors and printers. If they are unable to use these during school hours, they can often use them before or after school, at lunch, or during a study hall. Students who don't use computers at home can walk, take a bus, or have a parent drive them to a public library where computer access is free and often quite sophisticated. Their college professors and/or potential employers will expect work to be done in this way, so high school teachers needn't feel they are unduly burdening students by asking that final drafts be presented in this professional way. It is the right habit to get into.

In addition to the professional appearance of word-processed documents, various tools inside word processing programs and on the Internet can add visual appeal and sometimes enhance the meaning of writing. Integrating visual imagery either from word processing galleries or from Web-based sources can help students represent their work in striking ways. Varied fonts, colors, spacing, and the like can be used as tools for clarifying and enhancing meaning when done purposefully and not merely decoratively. Desktop publishing software can offer templates and heuristics helpful for layout and design of student publications. (See TopTenReviews, *desktop-publishing-software-review.toptenreviews.com*, for a list of desktop software programs at various price points. Many have student and educator discounts.) You will want to think carefully about how much of this kind of enhancement you will encourage in your students' writing.

In addition to the role that technology plays in how a final draft is presented, how and to whom their work gets presented has changed significantly in the last decade. Once the audience for a student writer was nearly always his or her class and their teacher. Today students share their writing on their own websites, on social networking sites (like *Facebook* and MySpace), through blogs, and as part of a number of different types of collaborations with other writers. They also read the work of other student writers in these ways and through collaborations with publishers and educational sources that host Web spaces for students to share their work and interact with other student writers. Computer technology has also presented new opportunities for students to write collaboratively. Large joint writing projects like Wikipedia (*www.wikipedia.org*) are opportunities for students to join their writing with the writing of people they will never meet to make all sorts of new meanings. This kind of group writing has benefits and drawbacks, each of which you can explore with your students. These mediums have various aspects that recommend them; as well as problems that classroom teachers will want to consider before allowing, mandating, or exploring these possibilities with students. Table 10.5 summarizes the characteristics in how writing is shared and responded to in these different mediums. Faster than we know, there will be new ways to present writing and new ways to find out the effect it has had on oth-

**TABLE 10.5. Technologies for Sharing Writing**

| Places to share writing | Characteristics | Resources |
| --- | --- | --- |
| Personal websites | Students can include their writing or links to other Web sources where their writing can be viewed. | *www.Web.com* <br> *stress.google.com* <br> *developer.apple.com/wwdc* |
| Blogs | Students can initiate blogs or respond to ideas in the blogs of others. These are often motivated by issues. | *www.blogger.com* <br> *www.google.com/accounts/ NewAccount?* <br> *www.blogstream.com* <br> *www.sampa.com* |
| Social networking sites | Students can share writing with small groups or with invited individuals. | *www.facebook.com* <br> *www.myspace.com* |
| Hosted websites | Students can upload their writing to locations set up by others. Often these are very large and include writing and responses to writing from children, adolescent, or adult writers; from professionals and students; from those wishing to share finished work; and from those wishing for feedback on in-process documents. | TeenLit: *www.teenlit.com* <br> Teen Ink: *teenink.com* <br> The Writer's Voice: *writers-voice.com/submission guidelines.html* <br> Young People's Press Online: *www.ypp.net/ submissionguidelines.asp* |
| "Wiki" writing | Named for the online collaborative encyclopedia project; collaborative writing with multiple contributors. | *www.wikipedia.org* |

*Note.* All retrieved April 25, 2008. Check all sites before referring students to ensure that they still exist in appropriate form.

**TABLE 10.6. Online Resources for Teachers Interested in Using Technology to Teach Writing**

| Source | Location | Description |
| --- | --- | --- |
| National Writing Project | *www.nwp.org/cs/public/ print/resource_topic/ writing_and_technology* | Dozens of short papers on all aspects of teaching writing with technology |
| Teaching Literature and Writing with Technology | *thwt.org/writingandlit.htm* | Many references from the center for teaching history through technology |
| Western Michigan University Center for Teaching English through Technology | *www.wmich.edu/teachenglish* | Links to resources for setting up e-communities, course websites, etc. |
| Purdue University Online Writing Lab | *owl.english.purdue.edu/owl/ resource/677/01* | One of the first and most comprehensive online writing labs. Follow links especially for grades 7–12 teachers. |

ers from locations near and far. This is an exciting prospect for writers and also for writing teachers. The authenticity of sharing writing with the world outside the classroom can be motivating and ultimately very satisfying for student writers. Once one starts writing and sharing with others outside the school community, writing becomes less something you do in school and more something you do as a writer.

Further resources for using technology to teach writing can be found in Table 10.6.

# Resources for Further Reading

## WRITING IN THE CONTENT AREAS

Friedman, A. A. (2000). Writing and evaluating assessments in the content area. *English Journal*, *90*(1), 107–116.

Gillis, C. (1997). *Writing outside the lines: Developing partnerships for writing.* Portsmouth, NH: Heinemann.

McKenna, M., & Robinson, R. (2005). *Teaching through text: Reading and writing in the content areas* (4th ed.). Upper Saddle River, NJ: Pearson Education.

Singer, J. (2006). *Stirring up justice: Writing and reading to change the world.* Portsmouth, NH: Heinemann.

Zemelman, S., Daniels, H., & Steineke, N. (2007). *Content-area writing: Every Teacher's guide.* Portsmouth, NH: Heinemann.

Zinsser, W. (2006). *Writing to learn.* New York: HarperCollins.

## WRITING IN VARIOUS GENRES

Burroway, J. (2002). *Writing fiction: A guide to narrative craft* (6th ed.). Boston: Addison-Wesley/Pearson Education.

Graham, R. (2006). *How to write fiction (and think about it).* Basingstoke, UK: Palgrave Macmillan.

Heard, G. (1989). *For the good of the earth and sun: Teaching poetry.* Portsmouth, NH: Heinemann.

Mackenzie, J. (2007). *Essay writing: Teaching the basics from the ground up.* York, ME: Stenhouse.

Mckee, R. (1997). *Story: Substance, structure, style and the principles of screenwriting*. New York: HarperCollins.

Murray, D. (1996). *Crafting a life in essay, story, poem*. Portsmouth, NH: Boynton/Cook.

Sipe, R. B., & Rosewarne, T. (2006). *Purposeful writing: Genre study in the secondary writing workshop*. Portsmouth, NH: Heinemann.

Zinsser, W. (Ed). (1998). *Inventing the truth: The art and craft of memoir*. New York: Houghton Mifflin.

## TRAITS OF WRITING

Berkow, P. F., & Berkow, A. J. (Producers). (2001). *English composition: Writing for an audience* (DVD). Washington, DC: Annenberg Media Learners.org.

Fletcher, R. (1993). *What a writer needs*. Portsmouth, NH: Heinemann.

Noppe-Brandon, G. (2004). *Find your voice: A methodology for enhancing literacy through re-writing and re-acting*. Portsmouth, NH: Heinemann.

Romano, T. (2004). *Crafting authentic voice*. Portsmouth, NH: Heinemann.

Umstatter, J. (1999).*Writing skills curriculum library: Ready-to-use prewriting and organization activities, unit 4*. Hoboken, NJ: Jossey-Bass.

## ASSESSMENT OF WRITING

Angelillo, J. (2005). *Writing to the prompt: When students don't have a choice*. Portsmouth, NH: Heinemann.

Gallagher, C. (2007). *Reclaiming assessment: A better alternative to the accountability agenda*. Portsmouth, NH: Heinemann.

Gradler, M. E., & Johnson, R. L. (2004). *Assessment in the literacy classroom*. Boston: Pearson Education.

Hill, B. C., Ruptic, C., & Norwick, L. (1998). *Classroom-based assessment*. Norwood, MA: Christopher-Gordon.

Porter, C., & Cleland, J. (1995). *The portfolio as a learning strategy*. Portsmouth, NH: Boynton/Cook.

Strickland, K., & Strickland, J. (1998). *Reflections on assessment: Its purposes, methods, and effects on learning*. Portsmouth, NH: Heinemann.

Tchudi, S. (Ed.). (1999). *Alternatives to grading student writing*. Urbana, IL: National Council of Teachers of English.

Wilson, M. (2006). *Rethinking rubrics in writing assessment*. Portsmouth, NH: Heinemann.

## WRITERS WRITING ABOUT WRITING

Erdrich, L. (1996). *The blue jay's dance*. New York: HarperAcademic.

Goldberg, N. (1986). *Writing down the bones: Freeing the writer within*. Boston: Shambhala

Hall, D. (1993). *Life work*. Boston: Beacon Press.

King, S. (2002). *On writing—A memoir of the craft*. New York: Simon & Schuster.

Lamott, A. (1995). *Bird by bird: Some instructions on writing and life*. New York: Knopf.

Murray, D. (1996). *Crafting a life in essay, story, poem*. New York: Boynton/Cook.

Rose, M. (1990). *Lives on the boundary*. New York: Penguin Books.

Ueland, B. (2007). *If you want to write: A book about art, independence, and spirit*. St. Paul, MN: Graywolf Press.

Welty, E. (2002). *On writing*. New York: Modern Library.

## TECHNOLOGY AND THE TEACHING OF WRITING

Goldberg, A., Russell, M., & Cook, A. (2003). The effect of computers on student writing: A meta-analysis of studies from 1992–2002. *Journal of Technology, Learning and Assessment, 2*(1), 1–51.

Karchmer-Klein, R. (2007). Best practices in using the Internet to support writing. In S. Graham, C. A. MacArthur, & J. Fitzgerald (Eds.), *Best practices in writing instruction* (pp. 222–241). New York: Guilford Press.

MacArthur, C. A. (2006). The effects of new technologies on writing and writing processes. In C. A. MacArthur, S. Graham, & J. Fitzgerald (Eds.), *Handbook of writing research* (pp. 248–262). New York: Guilford Press.

Moran, C. (2003). Computers and composition 1983–2002: What we have hoped for. *Computers and Composition, 20*(4), 343–359.

Warschauer, M. (2004). Technology and writing. In C. Davison & J. Cummins (Eds.), *Handbook of English language teaching*. Dordrecht, Netherlands: Kluwer.

# References

Andrews, R., Torgerson, C., Beverton, S., Freeman, A., Locke, T., Low, G., et al. (2006). The effect of grammar teaching on writing development. *British Educational Research Journal, 32*(1), 39–55.

Atwell, N. (1998). *In the middle: writing, reading, and learning with adolescents* (2nd ed.). Portsmouth, NH: Heinemann.

Bartholomae, D., & Petrosky, A. R. (Eds.). (1986). *Facts, artifacts, and counterfacts: Theory and method for a reading and writing course.* Upper Montclair, NJ: Boynton/Cook.

Beach, R., & Friedrich, T. (2006). Response to writing. In C. A. MacArthur, S. Graham, & J. Fitzgerald (Eds.), *Handbook of writing research* (pp. 222–234). New York: Guilford Press.

Bencich, C. B. (1999). Response: A promising beginning for learning to grade student writing. In S. Tchudi (Ed.), *Alternatives to grading student writing* (pp. 47–63). Urbana, IL: National Council of Teachers of English.

Berg, C. E. (1999). The effects of trained peer response on ESL students' revision types and writing quality. *Journal of Second Language Writing, 8*(3), 215–241.

Bisei, T., Brenner, D., McVee, M., Pearson, P. D., & Sarroub, L. K. (1997). Assessment in literature-based reading programs: Have we kept our promises? In T. Raphael & K. Au (Eds.), *Literature-based instruction: Reshaping the curriculum.* Norwood, MA: Christopher-Gordon.

Braddock, R., Lloyd-Jones, R., & Schoer, L. (1963). *Research in written composition.* Urbana, IL: National Council of Teachers of English.

Buehl, D. (2001). *Classroom strategies for interactive learning* (2nd ed.). Newark, DE: International Reading Association.

Calkins, L. M. (1983). *Lessons from a child: On the teaching and learning of writing.* Portsmouth, NH: Heinmann.

Calkins, L. M. (1994). *The art of teaching writing* (2nd ed.). Portsmouth, NH: Heinemann.

Calkins, L. M. (2006). *Units of study.* Portsmouth, NH: Heinemann.

Center for the Improvement of Early Reading Achievement. (1998). Every child a reader (online preview edition). Retrieved December 7, 2007, from *www. ciera.org/library/instresrc/ecr/ecrgoodies/ECR01-4.pdf.*

Collins, J. J. (1997). *Selecting and teaching focus correction areas: A planning guide.* Rowley, MA: The Network.

De La Paz, S., & Graham, S. (1997). Effects of dictation and advanced planning instruction on the composing of students with writing and learning problems. *Journal of Educational Psychology, 89,* 203–222.

Elbow, P. (1973). *Writing without teachers.* New York: Oxford University Press.

Elbow, P. (1981). *Writing with power.* New York: Oxford University Press.

Emig, J. (1971). *Composing process of twelfth graders.* Urbana, IL: National Council of Teachers of English.

Feng, S., & Powers, K. (2005). The short- and long-term effect of explicit grammar instruction on fifth graders' writing. *Reading Improvement, 42*(2), 67–72.

Fletcher, R. (1993). *What a writer needs.* Portsmouth, NH: Heinemann.

Fletcher, R. (1996). *A writer's notebook: Unlocking the writer within you.* New York: HarperCollins Publishers.

Fletcher, R. (2000). *How writers work: Finding a process that works for you.* New York: HarperCollins Publishers.

Fletcher, R. (2004). *Teaching the qualities of writing.* Portsmouth, NH: Heinemann.

Fletcher, R., & Portalupi, J. (1998). *Craft lessons: Teaching writing K–8.* York, ME: Stenhouse.

Fletcher, R., & Portalupi, J. (2001). *Writing workshop: The essential guide.* Portsmouth, NH: Heinemann.

Freedman, S. G. (1991). *Small victories: The real world of a teacher, her students, and their high school.* New York: HarperCollins.

Glynn, S. M., Britton, B. K., Muth, K. D., & Dogan, N. (1982). Writing and revising persuasive documents. *Journal of Educational Psychology, 74*(4) 557–567.

Goldberg, N. (1986). *Writing down the bones: Freeing the writer within.* Boston: Shambhala.

Graham, S., Harris, K. R., & Mason, L. H. (2005). Improving the writing performance, knowledge, and self-efficacy of struggling young writers: The effects of self-regulated strategy development. *Contemporary Educational Psychology, 30,* 207–241.

Graham, S., & Perin, D. (2007). *Writing next: Effective strategies to improve writing of adolescents in middle and high schools—A report to Carnegie Corporation of New York.* Washington, DC: Alliance for Excellent Education.

Graves, D. H. (1983). *Writing: Teachers and children at work.* Portsmouth, NH: Heinemann.

Graves, D. H. (1994). *A fresh look at writing.* Portsmouth, NH: Heinemann.

Greenwald, E. A., Persky, H. R., Campbell, J. R., & Mazzeo, J. (1999). National

Assessment of Educational Progress (NAEP) 1998 writing report card for the nation and the states. *Education Statistics Quarterly, 1*(4), 23–28.

Harris, J. (1990). The idea of community in the study of writing. In L. Ede (Ed.), *On writing research: The Braddock Essays* (pp. 260–272). Boston: Bedford.

Helfgott, D., & Westhaver, M. (2006a). Inspiration[(r)] software (Version 8.0) [Computer software]. Beaverton, OR: Inspiration Software.

Helfgott, D., & Westhaver, M. (2006b). Kidspiration[(r)] software (Version 2.1) [Computer software]. Beaverton, OR: Inspiration Software.

Hillocks, G., Jr. (1986). *Research on written composition: New directions for teaching.* Urbana, IL: National Council of Teachers of English.

Howie, S. M. H. (1979). A study: The effects of sentence combining practice on the writing ability and reading level of ninth-grade students. *Dissertation Abstracts International, 40*(1980-A). (University Microfilms No. 7923248).

Hughey, J. B., & Slack, C. (2001). *Teaching children to write: Theory into practice.* Upper Saddle River, NJ: Prentice Hall.

Hull, G., & Rose, M. (1989). Rethinking remediation: Toward a social-cognitive understanding of problematic reading and writing. *Written Communication, 8,* 139–154.

Kanella, R. J., (1997). The effects of discourse-function sentence combining on the expository writing of ninth graders. *Dissertation Abstracts International, Section A: The Humanities and Social Sciences, 58*(1), 112. University of Massachusetts, Lowell.

Lortie, D. C. (1975). *Schoolteacher: A sociological study.* Chicago: University of Chicago Press.

Macrorie, K. (1976). *Writing to be read.* Rochele Park, NJ: Hayden.

Murray, D. (1980). Writing as process: How writing finds its own meaning. In T. R. Donovan & B. W. McClelland (Eds.), *Eight approaches to teaching composition* (pp. 3–21). Urbana, IL: National Council of Teachers of English.

Murray, D. (1996). *A writer teaches writing* (rev. ed.) Portsmouth, NH: Boynton/ Cook.

National Council of Teachers of English. (1985). Grammar exercises to teach speaking and writing. Retrieved July 21, 2008, from *www.ncte.org/about/ over/positions/category/gram/107492.htm.*

National Writing Project. (n.d.). Retrieved August 16, 2007, from *www.writingproject.org.*

Pearson, P. D., & Gallagher, M. C. (1983). The instruction of reading comprehension. *Contemporary Educational Psychology, 8*(3), 317–344.

Rawlins, J. (2005). *The writer's way.* Boston: Houghton Mifflin.

Rose, M. (1989). *Lives on the boundary: A moving account of the struggles and achievements of America's educationally underprepared.* New York: Penguin Books.

Routman, R. (1991). *Invitations: Changing as teachers and learners, K–12.* Portsmouth, NH: Heinemann.

Routman, R. (1996). *Literacy at the crossroads: Crucial talk about reading, writing, and other teaching dilemmas.* Portsmouth, NH: Heinemann.

Schuster, E. H. (2004, January). National and state writing tests: The writing process betrayed. *Phi Delta Kappan, 85*(5), 375–378.

Sommers, N. (1982). Responding to student writing. *College Composition and Communication, 33*(2), 148–156.

Straub, R. (1997). Students' reactions to teacher comments: An exploratory study. *Research in the Teaching of English, 31*(1), 91–119.

Tchudi, S. (Ed.). (1999). *Alternatives to grading student writing.* Urbana, IL: National Council of Teachers of English.

Templeton, S. (2003). Spelling. In J. Flood, J. M. Jensen, D. Lapp, & J. R. Squire (Eds.), *Handbook of research on teaching the English language arts* (pp. 738–752). New York: Macmillan.

Tompkins, G. E. (2004). *Teaching writing: Balancing process and product.* Upper Saddle River, NJ: Pearson.

Trelease, J. (2001). *The read-aloud handbook* (5th ed.). New York: Penguin Books.

Troia, G., Graham, S., & Harris, K. R. (1999). The effects of teaching students with LD to plan mindfully when writing. *Exceptional Children, 65,* 235–252.

Weaver, C. (1996). *Teaching grammar in context.* Portsmouth: Heinemann.

Willey, R. J., & Berne, J. (1997). *Process of discovery: A writer's workshop.* New York: McGraw-Hill.

# Index

Page numbers in italics indicate tables or figures.